Hanging on Every Word

AN INTRODUCTION TO EXPOSITORY PREACHING

by
Paul N. Merideth

LOUISVILLE, KENTUCKY

Copyright © 2012
Paul N. Merideth
All rights reserved

All Scripture quotations, unless otherwise indicated, are taken from *The Holy Bible, English Standard Version*. Copyright 2001 by Crossway Bibles, a division of Good News Publishers. Used by permission. All rights reserved.

Cover design: Caleb Norris, Fine-Line Graphics
Editing: ChristianEditingServices.com
Production: Richard's Printery, 800 Cawthon St., Louisville, KY, United States, 40203.

ISBN: 978-0-615-66300-5

To the

Watterson Trail

CHURCH of CHRIST

in Louisville, Kentucky

for giving tremendous

encouragement and support

to a young preacher

TABLE OF CONTENTS

                                                    Page

Introduction 1

Chapter 1

Understanding Expository Preaching 5

Chapter 2

Defining Expository Preaching 13

Chapter 3

The Scriptural Mandate for Expository Preaching ... 19

Chapter 4

Preach the Word in Season and Out of Season 25

Chapter 5

Divine Revelation, Inspiration, and Authority 35

Chapter 6

Exegesis, Exposition, and Application of the Text .. 45

Chapter 7

A Suggested Sermon Delivery Model 53

Chapter 8

The Gospel Must Be Communicated
and a Response is Required. 59

Chapter 9

The Present Need for Expository Preaching. 71

Chapter 10

Conclusion. 79

Appendix 1

Verbal Illustrations and Devotionals. 81

Appendix 2

Sample Sermon. 117

Appendix 3

Bibliography. 127

HANGING ON EVERY WORD:

AN INTRODUCTION TO EXPOSITORY PREACHING

The craft of expository preaching must not be lost. When Hilkiah, the high priest, rediscovered the Book of the Law in the temple he immediately delivered it to the king. He knew something that should never have been forgotten had been lost. The king's reaction was startling: "When the king heard the words of the Book of the Law, he tore his clothes."[1] I suspect an emotional wave swept over King Josiah when he realized the Word of God had been neglected for decades. It is easy to imagine that, as he heard the Law being read, King Josiah hung eagerly on every word. These timeless truths of God had been lost in time, yet once they were re-engaged they went on to spark dramatic reform. Christian preachers must safeguard against the loss of God's Word by faithfully preaching the timeless truths of God in every generation. God has spoken and we hang on his every word.

It is my conviction that engaging expository preaching is the best, most effective form of gospel

---

[1] See 2 Kings 22:11 and its context for the full story.

God-glorifying preaching takes tremendous courage and faith. It is a sacred honor for the man of God to stand before an assembly and passionately, yet humbly, proclaim the truth of Scripture. We give thanks for gospel preachers who have faithfully marched the path to the pulpit in bygone years. We also rejoice that God continues to raise up proclaimers who step forward to speak His Word. My hope is that this book will promote interest in homiletics and provide encouragement to gospel preachers to "preach the Word."

Chapter 1
Understanding Expository Preaching

Phillip Brooks, in his seminal lecture on preaching, asserts there are two elements in preaching. He says, "Preaching is the communication of truth by man to men. It has in it two essential elements, truth and personality. Neither of those can it spare and still be preaching."[2] These two components of the preacher, his personality and his message, must converge to produce the preaching event. However, prior to that event, a complex system of processes occur that converge to make the preacher and his sermon unique. Furthermore, the undergirding philosophy from which he operates determines what nature his sermon will have. To understand expository preaching, that philosophy that includes one's view of inspiration, authority, and proclamation, must be explored.

The designation of "preacher" finds its root in the idea of a herald. A herald is one who announces the will of another. It pictures a representative from the king who is sent forth as messenger to speak on behalf of the ruler to the people. As the herald declares a royal edict, so the Christian preacher is one who heralds forth the will of God. The job of the messenger is not

---

[2] See Phillip Brooks' *Lectures on Preaching* presented at the Divinity School of Yale College in January and February of 1877.

to tamper with God's Word, but to announce it to the masses. This sentiment is expressed by the apostle Paul when he says that he "refused to tamper with God's word" because his duty was not to entice with words of persuasion but to proclaim the words of truth.[3]

This picture of the preacher as a "herald of God" is instructive. The Christian preacher must understand his duty is not to draw people to himself through sheer personal charisma alone, but to be a conduit of divine truth through the proclamation of God's Word. This principle embeds into the philosophy of preaching a healthy dose of humility. Preaching is not primarily about the preacher, but the message. Certainly, the character of the preacher is very important, and we cannot divorce the message from the messenger since both are intertwined in the preaching event. Also, the way the sermon is delivered is important. However, the first concern in our understanding of expository preaching is that the focus be on the content of the message. That content must be derived from Scripture.

This conviction means the preacher must engage with Scripture himself in a healthy way before he can ever aspire to declare it to the people. Hence, the preacher must be an exegete. The discipline of exegesis is the task of pulling out correct knowledge from the biblical text. It requires a careful reading and

---

[3] See 2 Corinthians 4:1-6.

interpretation of the text that seeks to identify the authorial meaning. For the preacher to be able to declare the message of God's Word, he must know the message to be declared. After all, as James Thompson says, "to preach is to speak for God."[4]

While the notion of the Christian preacher being a "herald of God" is instructive, we should note he is more than a herald. He has emerged from the assembly and is actively interacting with his listeners on an intimate, interpersonal communication level. The preacher is challenged to think beyond the formula of sermon construction and delivery. He is being asked to engage with the lasting repercussions of what he preaches and how God works in the protracted preaching event. Furthermore, this is more than just application of the sermon's message. Rather, it requires a networking of activities including revealing, preaching, listening, and living.[5]

This process also heightens the expectations of the preacher. Instead of delivering a sermon and being done, he should anticipate that God will act through the proclamation of Scripture. Michael Quicke, in emphasizing this point, says, "Since preaching moves in

---

[4] James W. Thompson, *Preaching Like Paul: Homiletical Wisdom for Today* (Louisville: Westminster / John Knox Press, 2001), 51.
[5] Michael J. Quicke, *360 Degree Preaching: Hearing, Speaking, and Living the Word* (Grand Rapids: Baker Academic, 2003), 51.

returning response to God, whose Word will not come back empty, we should expect things to happen."[6] There is power ascribed to Scripture. The Holy Spirit, working through the Bible, is God's chief agent of activity today and the way in which he speaks to the world. God is not aloof and disconnected from the world or from the preaching event. "His words in Scripture have broken the silence" and "preachers must realize that Scripture not only says things but also does things."[7]

Quicke, in his text *360 Degree Preaching*, wants preachers to remember the power of words and the presentation of those words to hearers. "Preaching has always lived in uneasy alliance with rhetoric."[8] Many critics of rhetorical preaching have "vehemently criticized rhetoric as dangerously manipulative," but the practical reality is that "words always have a capacity to persuade," and "what matters is whether it is ethical or unethical persuasion."[9] We preach God's words with legitimate persuasion, trusting in the Lord rather than in the charisma of the preacher. Henry Ward Beecher classically explains:

---

[6]Ibid.
[7]Ibid, 53.
[8]Ibid, 54.
[9]Ibid, 55.

Eloquence has been defined, sometimes, as the art of moving men by speech. Preaching has this additional quality, that it is the art of moving men from a lower to a higher life. It is the art of inspiring them to a nobler manhood.[10]

An important regulating factor about rhetoric is that the preacher must have authentic humility. He should be submissive before the Lord and His Word, not arrogant or prideful. The preacher must remember that humility is to always be imbedded within his identity. Richard Baxter, the Puritan preacher, said: "I preach as never sure to preach again, and as a dying man to dying men." The classic statement on preaching from Phillip Brooks further highlights the communication aspect of preaching that is reliant upon the preacher's personality.

> What, then, is preaching, of which we are to speak? It is not hard to find a definition. Preaching is the communication of truth by man to men. It has in it two essential elements, truth and personality. Neither of those can it spare and still be preaching. The truest truth, the most authoritative statement of God's will, communicated in any other way than through the personality of brother man to men is not preached truth.[11]

---

[10] Henry Ward Beecher. *Yale Lectures on Preaching* (1892).
[11] See Phillip Brooks' *Lectures on Preaching* (1898).

In preaching, the preacher manages *logos* (content), *pathos* (emotion), and *ethos* (character). Since it involves the culmination of a complex system of processes, "the way in which preachers use words requires urgent care and attention today."[12]

I advocate a full-orbed understanding and appreciation of expository preaching. I believe an operating philosophy that pulls together a complex system of processes needs to be constantly affirmed. There is a present need to promote a philosophy that approaches the homiletic task with seriousness, a high view of Scripture, and a commitment to authentic application that fosters positive spiritual repercussions. This rock solid philosophical commitment to the true nature of Scripture and engaging exposition will ensure the preacher comes at his task with diligence. In lamenting the prevalence of shallow preaching, Tom Holland warns that "a wealth of technique cannot compensate for a poverty of content."[13]

Hence, the preacher is to be committed to biblical scholarship. After all, the true purpose of rigorous theological study is exposition. Karl Barth rightly asserts "theology as a church discipline ought in all its branches to be nothing other than sermon

---

[12]Quicke, *360 Degree Preaching*, 55.
[13]Thomas H. Holland, *Encouraging Expository Preaching* (Brentwood: Penmann Books, 2000), 57.

preparation."[14] Furthermore, in his textbook on biblical hermeneutics, Grant Osborne, in speaking of expository preaching, says:

> It is my contention that the final goal of hermeneutics is not systematic theology but the sermon. The actual purpose of Scripture is not explanation but exposition, not description but proclamation. God's Word speaks to every generation, and the relationship between meaning and significance summarizes the hermeneutical task. It is not enough to recreate the original intended meaning of a passage. We must elucidate its significance for our day.[15]

Therefore, expository preaching is a vital and necessary skill that all faithful Christian preachers must develop.

What I stress, throughout this book, is the superiority of the expository preaching philosophy. This claim is formulated based on the reality of divine revelation. God has acted via speech, and the Bible is His Word to humanity. The role of preacher is part of God's plan for the ongoing declaration of His Word to the world. Therefore, preachers recognize their mission to act as a herald for the King. Furthermore, the preacher takes up the task of effective communicator.

---

[14]Karl Barth, *Homiletics* (Louisville: Westminster / John Knox Press, 1991), 17.
[15]Grant R. Osborne, *The Hermeneutical Spiral* (Downers Grove: IVP Academics, 2006), 29.

Expository preaching involves the synthesis of complex processes. We mine the biblical text for meaning, we artfully craft it into a sermon, and we preach it with persuasion.

Chapter 2
Defining Expository Preaching

John Stott contends "all true Christian preaching is expository preaching."[16] He calls for preachers to anchor their sermon content in Scripture. However, definitions of expository preaching come in all sizes. Some are extensive, seeking to include detailed nuances defining the boundaries of what is and is not expository preaching. Others offer a minimalist definition that captures the concept using only its irreducible parts. To handle this reality of diverse definitions, this study will gently engage with just a sampling of what is available on the subject.

Because it appears extensively throughout preaching literature, we begin with Haddon Robinson's definition of expository preaching. Robinson defines expository preaching as "the communication of a biblical concept, derived from and transmitted through a historical, grammatical, and literary study of a passage in its context, which the Holy Spirit first applies to the personality and experience of the preacher, then through him to his hearers."[17] The five key elements in

---

[16] John Stott, *Between Two Worlds: The Challenge of Preaching Today* (Grand Rapids: Eerdmans Pub. Co., 1982), 125.
[17] Haddon W. Robinson, *Biblical Preaching: The Development and Delivery of Expository Messages*, 2nd ed. (Grand Rapids: Baker Academic, 2001), 22.

Robinson's definition are 1) the passage governs the sermon, 2) the expositor communicates a concept, 3) the concept comes from the text, 4) the concept is first applied to the expositor, and 5) the concept is next applied to the hearers. Robinson's definition warrants respect and functions as an extremely helpful schematic. However, while there is indeed a methodology to the procedure, expository preaching is to be best understood not as a technique for sermon construction, but as a philosophy that guides the preacher's thinking for sermon development. Robinson says, "expository preaching at its core is more a philosophy than a method."[18]

Hershael York's call for "engaging exposition" strikes a needed balance wherein the text is highly regarded yet audience application is also a crucial factor. After all, "sermons are not about just imparting information."[19] For the preacher practicing "engaging exposition" "his passion must be to preach the Word in such a way that he accurately teaches the meaning of the text and leads his audience to discover its implications for their life situations so they respond in obedience and become more like Christ as a result."[20]

---

[18] Robinson, *Biblical Preaching*, 20.

[19] Hershael W. York and Bert Decker, *Preaching With Bold Assurance: A Solid and Enduring Approach to Engaging Exposition* (Nashville: B&H Pub., 2003), 11.

[20] York, *Preaching With Bold Assurance*, 15.

Thus, "expository preaching is any kind of preaching that shows people the meaning of a biblical text and leads them to apply it to their lives."[21]

Floyd Bresee says that "expository preaching is preaching based upon a significant Bible passage so that the sermon's principal lessons originate in Scripture and are applied to a present need."[22]

Merrill Unger put it this way: "What saith the Lord 'is the alpha and the omega' of expository preaching. It begins in the Bible and ends in the Bible and all that intervenes springs from the Bible. In other words, expository preaching is Bible-centered preaching."[23]

Bryan Chapell summarizes a host of definitions by saying it is only expository preaching when "it expound(s) Scripture by deriving from a specific text main points and subpoints that disclose the thought of the author, cover the scope of the passage, and are applied to the lives of the listeners."[24]

One final sampling comes from Jerry Vines and Jim Shaddix in their text *Power in the Pulpit*, where expository preaching is defined as "a discourse that expounds a passage of Scripture, organizes it around a

---

[21]Ibid, 33.
[22]Floyd Bresee, "Expository Preaching" *Ministry Magazine* (1955; Digitally Reprinted, 1994).
[23]Merril Unger, *Principles of Expository Preaching* (Grand Rapids: Zondervan, 1974).
[24]Bryan Chapell, *Christ-Centered Preaching: Redeeming the Expository Sermon* (Grand Rapids: Baker Books, 1994), 129.

central theme and main divisions which issue forth from the given text, and then decisively applies its message to the listeners."[25]

It is beyond the scope of this study to explore fully all the nuances of defining expository preaching. Hence, for our purposes, I offer a moderately simple definition: *Expository preaching is the coherent proclamation of biblical truth for the purpose of faith development with special emphasis on the scriptural grounding for the sermon focus and the encouraging of truth application to the listener.*

This definition implicitly asserts there is a link between the form of the text and the form of the sermon. However, it is not feasible to always conform the shape of the sermon to the text. After all, our reading of the text is cross-cultural. In essence, a dynamic equivalent – there's truth here and we can't say it just exactly the way they said it, so we deliver it into our context and culture. However, to stray too far from the text leads to bad things happening in the sermon. Therefore, the expository preaching philosophy is a necessary anchor that holds the sermon to reasonable parameters of orthodoxy.

Just as God revealed his Word in a variety of genres and styles, so also contemporary preaching

---

[25] Jerry Vines and Jim Shaddix, *Power in the Pulpit: How to Prepare and Deliver Expository Sermons* (Chicago: Moody Press, 1999), 29.

comes in a variety of forms. Indeed, there are boundaries to expository preaching that when crossed, cripples the confidence of the sermon. But, within the legitimate scope of expository preaching a range of forms, styles, deliveries, and techniques exist. Defining these boundaries and cataloging these forms paves the way forward for advancing the conversation on expository preaching.

Chapter 3
The Scriptural Mandate for Expository Preaching

Preaching is not an optional activity. The Christian church is solemnly tasked with the duty of gospel proclamation in every generation. Thankfully, God has provided enduring source material for the preaching enterprise so the practice of gospel preaching will never be lost. However, for the Christian preacher, the Bible constitutes not only the content of what is to be preached, but also the philosophy of preaching itself. From the Old Testament tradition of the proclaiming prophet[26] to the New Testament evangelist, the preacher is to be a man of God who steps forward with a message to declare. The Bible lays a heavy responsibility on the message bearer to speak divine truth to the world. It gives explicit direction for the preacher to "preach the word."[27]

In order to develop a healthy understanding of expository preaching, we need first to engage with the New Testament portrait of preaching. Jesus Christ, the

---

[26] As an example of prophetic passion for preaching notice Jeremiah 20:8,9: "For whenever I speak, I cry out, I shout, 'Violence and destruction!' For the word of the LORD has become for me a reproach and a derision all day long. If I say, 'I will not mention him, or speak any more in his name,' there in my heart as it were a burning fire shut up in my bones, and I am weary with holding it in, and I cannot."

[27] 2 Timothy 4:2.

incarnate God, was a preacher.[28] We read of Jesus' readiness to preach throughout all four gospel accounts. He preaches the message of God's kingdom and calls listeners to respond to Himself as the true Messiah. Preachers must look to Jesus not only as the core content of their preaching material, but also as their example of declaring God's truth. Hugo McCord, in his chapter on "Jesus As an Example for Preachers," illustrates this point: "A boy will not stumble as much when he puts his feet in his father's snow-tracks. So a preacher, when he steadily keeps his eyes on Jesus, will stumble less."[29] We should be careful not to push this too far since we can never preach as the Son of God. Nevertheless, we observe the worth of a preaching ministry.

The New Testament epistles also show Christian men who are preeminently focused on preaching. For example, the Apostle Paul evidenced tremendous passion for preaching Jesus Christ and Him crucified:[30] the gospel message of Jesus' death, burial, and resurrection.[31] Throughout the Pauline letters and much of the book of Acts, we see the work and evangelism of the Apostle Paul. His preaching is

---

[28] Consider Mark 1:14-15, 38-39 and its context. See also Luke 4:17-21 and consider it possibly being Jesus' "preaching ministry mission statement."
[29] Hugo McCord, 23
[30] 1 Corinthians 2:2.
[31] 1 Corinthians 15:1-4.

markedly characterized by a bold declaration of truth. In the letters of Paul, there is no indication that his evangelistic preaching involved allowing the listeners to set the agenda for his message. From Paul's perspective, their misguided religious ways consisted of hopelessness[32] and enslavement to idols[33] with out-of-control emotions.[34] Therefore, instead of soothing his listeners, he issued a challenge to their belief system. He did this because evangelistic preaching always culminates in a call for the listeners to turn from the old existence of error to a new life that is determined not by subjective feelings or sensitivity, but by Jesus Christ and His truth.

Evangelistic preaching calls for a decision. Most of Paul's listeners did not respond favorably to his preaching. He often cramped the feelings, sensitivities, and egos of hearers. Furthermore, by refusing to treat the gospel as merchandise[35] or to tamper with God's Word,[36] Paul demonstrated his concern to be faithful to his divine commission, even if his faithfulness produced few results. Paul gave his listeners a clear choice, a message they could reject - and most of them

---

[32] 1 Thessalonians 4:18.
[33] See 1 Thessalonians 1:9; 1 Corinthians 12:2; and Galatians 4:3,8.
[34] See 1 Thessalonians 4:5.
[35] See 2 Corinthians 2:17.
[36] See 2 Corinthians 4:2.

did.[37] The preaching of the Apostle Paul focused on divine truth. In Galatians 1:6-10, Paul speaks in an aggressive tone in order to convey a very serious message. He warns that a "different gospel" has been preached by some who have distorted the true gospel of Christ. This unfortunate reality results in Paul employing judgment language that calls down a curse on those who have failed to be faithful in the teaching and telling of the gospel.

Gospel loyalty is an important matter for the entire church, but especially crucial for preachers. The preacher must take care not to alter the gospel. Today there is tremendous pressure to water down its mandates and make them more palatable for the contemporary crowd. So what makes tweaking the gospel message so bad as to warrant Paul's rough speaking in his letter to the Galatians? Well, just as tampering with the delicate inner workings of electronic devices will void the warranty, tampering with the gospel distorts it and voids it of divine power.[38] Since the power of God to save is coupled

---

[37]For a fuller exploration of this theme in Paul's preaching see James Thompson's text *Preaching Like Paul*. Louisville: Westminster / John Knox Press, 2001.
[38]The Apostle Paul criticized this very thing in Galatians 1:6-11. See also Romans 1:16,17 where the gospel contains God's power to save. Hence, when we change the gospel message we separate it from that divine salvific effectiveness.

22

with the gospel, the preacher risks divesting the gospel of its salvific effectiveness by changing the message. Preachers must honor fidelity to the gospel message because it is the gospel that saves. It is God through the gospel, not the preacher, who transforms lives.

When it comes to gospel proclamation, the mission of preaching is to faithfully convey the saving gospel of Jesus Christ and call for a response. From Paul's perspective, misguided religious ways bring hopelessness. Therefore, instead of soothing his listeners, he issued a challenge to their belief system. Evangelistic preaching always calls listeners to embrace change and allow Jesus Christ and His truth to enact transformation.

The scriptural mandate for expository preaching is arrived at by understanding what the Bible says about preaching as a whole. Throughout the canon, stress is put on the notion that the preacher is but the conduit for relaying God's message. Since God has revealed His message in the form of Scripture, we must, therefore, manage the material with care. Even the details matter, since each syllable is God's. The preacher must submit to the authority of the Bible. In preaching, the mandate is to speak forth God's meaning, derived from His Word, contextualized to the contemporary hearers, and spoken with humble confidence. Stephen McQuoid puts it this way: "The job of the preacher is to declare 'thus saith the Lord.' What we preach is not a matter of opinion, neither is it something that can be negotiated. The Word of God is to be obeyed."[39] It must be preached because, without revelation reaching their lives, humanity has no hope.

Therefore, since the message preached is the Word of God, preachers must study it, preach it, and labor over it, giving their best to present it faithfully to the world. Furthermore, the preacher must authentically live out the mandates of God's Word. These are the inescapable implications of divine revelation. Since God has truly spoken through his Word, then we are obligated to listen, obey, and then proclaim.

---

[39]Stephen McQuoid, *The Beginner's Guide to Expository Preaching* (Great Britain: Christian Focus Pub., 2002), 21.

Chapter 4
Preach the Word in Season and Out of Season

In his instruction to his fellow minister Timothy, the apostle Paul expresses "the preacher's assignment." He writes these inspired words to the young preacher:

> I charge you in the presence of God and of Christ Jesus, who is to judge the living and the dead, and by his appearing and his kingdom: preach the word; be ready in season and out of season; reprove, rebuke, and exhort, with complete patience and teaching. For the time is coming when people will not endure sound teaching, but having itching ears they will accumulate for themselves teachers to suit their own passions, and will turn away from listening to the truth and wander off into myths. As for you, always be sober-minded, endure suffering, do the work of an evangelist, fulfill your ministry.[40]

This is the most instructive biblical passage for the work of expository preaching. The Greek phrase κήρυξον τὸν λόγον, "preach the word," in verse two conveys a solemn charge wherein Timothy is commissioned to proclaim God's insripturated truth. The phrase is set up in verse one not only by the commission διαμαρτύρομαι, a present middle indicative

---
[40] 2 Timothy 4:1-5 as rendered from the 2001 English Standard Version.

first person deponent singular from διαμαρτύρομαι meaning "charge, warn, adjure," but also by an accusative in oaths ἐνώπιον τοῦ θεοῦ καὶ Χριστοῦ Ἰησοῦ, "in the presence of God and Christ Jesus." This language of a formulaic oath illustrates the seriousness of the imperative. The construct and context of the phrase κήρυξον τὸν λόγον[41] in 2 Timothy 4:2 further intimates the imperative to "preach" is to have priority force. Wallace remarks, as a constative aorist imperative, "this command says nothing about beginning or continuing an action. It basically has the force of, 'Make this your top priority.'"[42] Hence, for Paul to craft his imperative to "preach the word" with a set-up charge and oath, and to follow it with a vivid call to implement the command no matter the circumstance, we, therefore, rightly place tremendous emphasis on the preaching mandate. For Paul nothing was more serious than the task of preaching the Word of God. In his text *Preaching Like Paul*, James Thompson speaks not only of the serious task preachers have of communicating God's Word, but also the need for hearers to take seriously their duty as well.

---

[41] κήρυξον is a first aorist active imperative of κηρύσσω. τὸν λόγον is accusative masculine singular from λόγος. Also, for "the word" used absolutely, see 1 Thessalonians 1:6 and Galatians 6:6.

[42] Daniel B. Wallace, *Greek Grammar Beyond the Basics: An Exegetical Syntax of the New Testament* (Grand Rapids: Zondervan, 1996), 721.

In recalling his preaching as God's word, Paul places his preaching in proper perspective and invites his listeners to recognize the difference between preaching and all other forms of discourse. The community needs to recognize that preaching is a trust and that the preacher's task is to act as trustee of the message on God's behalf (1 Thess. 2:4-5). Paul's reminder of his own preaching as a trust actually instructs the congregation in how to listen to a sermon and what to expect of other preachers. The task of preacher is to confront the congregation with God's own words as they are mediated in scripture.[43]

The commission to "preach the word" brings to bear a full force imperative to make preaching the priority. Herein is an important lesson for those in preaching ministry. The hectic pace of a church office can sometimes distract and deflect the preacher from his ministry of the Word.[44] The pastoral duties of member management and administration can quickly consume gross amounts of day and night. Therefore, time for prayer and sermon preparation must be safeguarded.

More than anything else, the preacher must be able to preach. His preaching should reflect a passion,

---

[43] James W. Thompson, *Preaching Like Paul: Homiletical Wisdom for Today* (Louisville: Westminster / John Knox Press, 2001), 51.
[44] See Acts 6:2-4 and its context.

priority, and urgency that fulfill the mandate of κήρυξον τὸν λόγον. To preach is "to make public declarations, proclaim aloud," "to announce or make known," especially a message "of a transcendent nature."[45] A preacher is pictured as "an official entrusted with a proclamation," "a herald."[46] Thus, the idea of *preach* entails the deliberate declaration of an event.[47]

The message that is to be communicated by the preacher is "the Word." This is none other than God's Word that He has spoken through the vehicle of inspiration. John Stott clarifies by saying, "Paul does not need to specify it further, for Timothy will know at once that it is the body of doctrine which he has heard from Paul and which Paul has now committed to him to pass on to others. It is identical with 'the deposit' of chapter 1. And in this fourth chapter it is equivalent to 'the sound teaching' (3), 'the truth' (4) and 'the faith' (7)."[48]

In Stott's commentary, he adds this "same charge is laid upon the church of every age. We have no liberty to invent our message, but only to communicate 'the

---

[45] Frederick William Danker, ed. *A Greek-English Lexicon of the New Testament and other Early Christian Literature*, 3rd ed. (Chicago: Univ. of Chicago Press, 2000), 543.
[46] Ibid.
[47] Gerhard Friedrich, *Theological Dictionary of the New Testament*, ed. Gerhard Kittel, vol. 3 (Grand Rapids: Eerdmans, 1965), 703.
[48] John R.W. Stott, *The Message of 2 Timothy* (Downers Grove: Inter-Varsity Press, 1973), 106.

word' which God has spoken and has now committed to the church as a sacred trust."[49] The Christian preacher must be ready to proclaim the Word of God whether or not circumstances are favorable, whether or not the audience is receptive.

Thus, this solemn charge to preach the Word is framed by the impetus to do so no matter the circumstances. It's interesting that the apostle's passionate command to "preach the word" is closely wed with the urgency to "be ready in season and out of season." This "out of season" preaching command has powerful breadth. With this circumstance parameter ("in season and out of season") installed onto the imperative ("preach the word"), the force of *preach* sweeps over the horizon of history.

There is glorious power intimately connected with the preaching of the Word. This power is to be allowed to break into any time. Thus, it has an "ahistorical" quality. Timeless truth must be told.

Notice also the phrase ἐπίστηθι εὐκαίρως ἀκαίρως, "in season and out of season." The term ἀκαίρως carries the notion of "untimely"[50] or "out of time." Certainly, in context, Paul is advancing the mandate to preach no matter the circumstance. The Word is to be

---

[49]Ibid.
[50]Frederick William Danker, ed. *A Greek-English Lexicon of the New Testament and other Early Christian Literature*, 3rd ed., 34.

proclaimed when it's convenient or inconvenient, when the hearers want to listen and when they don't. The truth of God is to be declared regardless of comfort level.

This phrase, "in season and out of season," has an interesting look and the idea of "out of time" preaching has a compelling connotation. The reason the Word is to be preached no matter the circumstance is due to its timeless truth nature. So the preacher is to be ready. That is, he stands on the edge, ready to spring into proclamation. When he speaks forth the Word of Truth, he is uttering speech that breaks into time and space. This "in-breaking" of divine truth through the preaching of Scripture is unique in human discourse.

Additionally, it needs to be acknowledged that the theme of preaching is a major motif in the New Testament. There is tremendous scriptural content about what is to be preached and the attitude of the preacher. While it is beyond the scope of this study to engage rigorously with every New Testament passage on preaching, it nevertheless is helpful to quickly chart some of the key passages that speak of preaching. This simple list of some of the passages wherein the New Testament peculiarly speaks of preaching offers a sampling of this major motif.

- "Proclaiming the gospel of God" is the chief ministry. Jesus himself preached "the kingdom of God is at hand; repent and believe in the gospel."[51]
- The apostles delegated various ministry duties so that they themselves could be devoted to "the ministry of the word."[52]
- Preaching is presented as an integral cog in the mechanism of connecting people to faith: "how are they to hear without someone preaching?"[53]
- Since Scripture is "breathed out by God" and is able to equip "for every good work," it must therefore be proclaimed regardless of cultural circumstance.[54]
- The gospel message, faithfully conveyed through the preacher, is in reality "the word of God."[55]
- The preaching of "Christ crucified" uniquely and transcendently contains the "power of God."[56]
- Preachers should not "tamper with God's word" but instead proclaim "Jesus Christ as Lord."[57]
- The proclamation of Jesus is to be the centerpiece of sermon content so the hearer will "mature in Christ."[58]

---

[51] Mark 1:14,15.
[52] Acts 6:4.
[53] Romans 10:13-17.
[54] 2 Timothy 3:16-4:5.
[55] 1 Thessalonians 2:13.
[56] 1 Corinthians 1:18-2:14.
[57] 2 Corinthians 4:1-6.
[58] Colossians 1:28,29

- Preacher training should be generationally propagated so "faithful men" will "be able to teach others also."[59]
- God's "oracles" arrive via the ministry of preaching "by the strength that God supplies" for the glorification of God "through Jesus Christ."[60]

These samplings of instructional passages on preaching demonstrate it has a primary role in the ongoing life of the church. The preaching of God's Word in the ecclesial context should not be assumed, minimized, or relegated to something that is merely tolerated. Rather, preaching has a glorious tradition and ongoing function that has enduring relevance in the world.

In Second Timothy, after the Apostle Paul speaks of the inspired origin of Scripture,[61] he turns to the matter of declaring God's Word. The preacher is to "preach the word"[62] being faithful in proclamation when it is convenient and when it is not. The preacher is to reprove, rebuke, and exhort from God's Word when the people in the pew want to hear it and when they do not. It is to be done with humility and the patient promotion of healthy doctrine. On occasion some may accuse: "Well, you preachers sure think a lot

---

[59] 2 Timothy 2:2.
[60] 1 Peter 4:11.
[61] 2 Timothy 3:16,17.
[62] 2 Timothy 4:2.

of yourselves." Our unpretentious reply is, "No, we think a lot of the Word." There will be occasions when hearers will not want to be exposed to the Word of God because of interference from sin, but the preacher who is faithful in his ministry is nonetheless devoted to the divine call to preach the Word of God.[63]

---

[63] 2 Timothy 4:3-8.

Chapter 5
Divine Revelation, Inspiration, and Authority

True gospel preachers accept the entire canon of Scripture as nothing less than God's Word written. Two prerequisite components for developing a viable philosophy of expository preaching are 1) the principle of divine special revelation and 2) the affirmation of inherent authority in the text. Because the Bible is from God, it radiates intrinsic relevance and it stands alone as our source of authority for what we declare. For the preacher to faithfully proclaim the Word of God, he must exegete the text and convey authorial meaning[64] in a homiletic format. In summary, the preacher is to "preach the word" because it really is the Word of God.

If God truly has spoken in Scripture, then all human beliefs, ideas, and philosophies are subject to its judgments. However, if the Bible is not of divine origin, then it is just one of many humanistic perspectives on reality. Everything hangs or falls on the

---

[64]For discussions related to the importance of "meaning" see: Robert H. Stein, *A Basic Guide to Interpreting the Bible: Playing by the Rules* (Grand Rapids: Baker Books, 1994), 38. See also E.D. Hirsch, *Validity in Interpretation*, (New Haven: Yale Univ. Press, 1967). See also Grant Osbourne's "meaning-significance format" discussed in the introduction of his text *The Hermeneutical Spiral*, (Downers Grove: IVP Academic, 2006). These scholars rightly contend that meaning is set by the biblical Author/authors.

strength of divine special revelation.

A valid theology of Christian preaching accepts the Bible as the authoritative revelatory Word of God. Authority is inherent in the text because of divine inspiration. This inspiration of Scripture means Spirit-moved men wrote God-breathed words which are divinely authoritative for Christian faith and practice.[65] The implication is the inherent authority of the scriptural text. God has revealed himself and because the Bible is God's Word, it has the right to speak authoritatively to every people of every era. N.T. Wright articulates it well when he says the phrase "authority of scripture" "can make Christian sense only if it is a shorthand for the authority of the triune God, exercised somehow through scripture."[66] I would strengthen the "somehow" to be the actual text itself. God has set the meaning we access by understanding the text. Thus, there is authority in every word because every word is God-inspired. That's why we hang on every word – because every word of scripture is God-planned, God-provided, and God-powerful.

True Christian preaching must find its grounding

---

[65] The grounding for this high view of Scripture may be established from Deuteronomy 29:29; 2 Timothy 3:16,17; and 2 Peter 1:20,21. Additionally, external evidence for biblical inspiration exists but that material is beyond the scope of this study.

[66] N.T. Wright, *Scripture and the Authority of God: How to Read the Bible Today* (New York: Harper Collins Pub., 2011), 21.

in the Word of God. In developing a healthy understanding of expository preaching, the preacher needs to affirm this high view of Scripture. If the preacher does not begin with a proper understanding of the inspiration of Scripture, the entire course of his approach to preaching will be charted in a radically different way. The Bible itself declares itself to be of divine origin. Approximately 3,800 times in the Old and New Testaments there is some formula of "thus says the Lord." The some forty writers of Holy Scripture produced their work, not due to their own cleverness, but by inspiration of God. In 2 Timothy 3:16, the Apostle Paul declares "all scripture is given by inspiration of God." The word rendered "inspiration" carries with it the idea of "God-breathed" or "from the very mouth of God." God worked directly through the writers of the Bible to inscripturate His revealed will. Inspiration means Spirit-moved men wrote God-breathed words that are divinely authoritative for Christian faith and practice. In 2 Peter 1:20-21, the apostle Peter elaborates on the mechanics of the process as he asserts that the writers of Scripture were "carried along" as they were moved by the Holy Spirit. Just as a leaf is blown by the wind, so also the writers of the Bible were guided and superintended by the Holy Spirit to record just what God wanted written without omission or addition. The Apostle Paul, in his correspondence to the church in Thessalonica, commends them for recognizing Scripture not as the will of men, but as it really is: the Word of God.[67] The mystery of inspiration is that God allowed the writer's own personality and vocabulary to remain, while divinely superintending their work. Thus, the Bible, as the supreme source material for all Christian preaching, is not a product of the will of men. Rather, the Word of God represents divine revelation wherein God used the agency of inspiration to declare His specific will to the world. The Bible is unique and stands alone as an authoritative source of spiritual truth. This conviction that the Bible is the Word of God is the necessary starting point for developing a theology of preaching that informs a proper philosophy of expository preaching.

An additional point to make pertains to the idea that the preacher is managing eternal truth material. Truth must be rightly handled.[68] Preaching occurs in the context of history, but there is peculiar truth content that transcends time. Preaching as timeless truth-telling is a paradigm that tasks the preacher with faithfully proclaiming the eternal word of God, in the fluid contemporary setting. The preacher is to humbly recognize his role as a timeless truth-teller who

---

[67]See 1 Thessalonians 2:13 and its context.
[68]2 Timothy 2:15.

proclaims unchanging divine realities. My son is seven years old and weighs fifty-four pounds. Those are true statements. However, with passing time, and continued normal development, they will no longer be true, but will become inaccurate, and thus false. The divine timeless truths we have in view, however, are ones immune to time and development.

When we preach, we tap into those perennial truth realities that mix into our contextualized speaking. Those timeless truths are like the eggs in a recipe. They are stirred into the mix, serve an integral cohesive role, and become part of the whole. Likewise, when we rightly locate the "eternal truth component" of a passage, its nature is such that it takes on a timeless relevancy. When proclaimed in contextualized language form and in logical thought order, this component acts as a universal reality that reaches into the faith community through the sermon and impacts hearts. The timeless truth portion of preaching is the same throughout time – just as eggs are always eggs. However, eggs have been used to make many different kinds of foods. The preacher surrounds the timeless truth of the sermon with contextualized speaking the hearers receive and apply. This is a potentially helpful perspective because it stimulates the realization that there is otherworldly truth engulfed within the sermon. When the preacher truly believes preaching echoes the truths of God, the man in the pulpit is infused with awe which then migrates to the people in the pew. This perspective, when dovetailed with an honoring of the biblical text and submission to its inherent authority, offers a helpful homiletic cognizance. The preacher remembers, within his biblical sermon, there is power to change lives.

Furthermore, Jesus himself embodies divine incarnational truth. As a man, he lived in historical, cultural, and spatial context. Yet, in his divinity, He embodied timeless truth. When Pilate asked Jesus, "What is truth,"[69] he failed to realize truth was an arm's length away. Similarly, the sermon contains timeless truth in the body of contextualized speaking. Michael Quicke unpacks the idea of "incarnational preaching" when he says:

> Because the gospel's truth and experience reside in the person of Jesus, his big story or 'grand narrative' remains constant even though human cultures continually shift and the story is heard in different ways. Telling God's timeless story in our time remains the critical task for all preachers everywhere. The other main timeless truth is that humankind need salvation.[70]

---

[69] John 18:37,38.
[70] Michael Quicke, *360 Degree Preaching*, 24-25.

When the timeless truths of God's Word are appropriately preached, they have the potential to display the irreducible parts of faith. They are the DNA of the Christian religion. These simple yet profound truth realities issue a clarion call to encounter God and learn core spiritual content. In preaching, the homilitician showcases these fundamentals to hearers.

Hearers need to be confronted with these perennial divine realities in order to jar them from short focus terrestrial living. "Set your minds on things that are above, not on things that are on earth."[71] The herald of God must understand his duty is not to draw people to himself through sheer personal charisma alone, but to be a conduit of divine truth through the proclamation of God's Word.

This concept embeds into his philosophy of preaching a healthy dose of humility, knowing the truth does not originate from his own cleverness. Rather, when he preaches timeless truth, it becomes like a brick crashing through glass. There is an in-breaking of divine truth spoken into a finite world with demonstrable results. So, while the preacher is humbled in knowing he is but a conduit of something celestially dramatic, he also takes confidence in the fact that eternal truths of God are working themselves into the consciousness of those who listen. This in-working has

---

[71] Colossians 3:2.

the potential to foster faith.[72] In preaching "we refuse to practice cunning or to tamper with God's word"[73] because "we have this treasure in jars of clay, to show that the surpassing power belongs to God and not to us."[74] This has historically been the conviction of all faithful gospel preachers, and it is an ideological legacy that must continue.

In summary, a high view of Scripture that affirms divine revelation and inspiration brings weighty implications upon the task of Christian preaching. The entire structure of Christian preaching is framed by the Word of God because it is God's own self-disclosure. For the preacher, this collection of sixty-six inspired books compiled into the one text we call the Bible constitutes the chief authoritative source material for the preaching enterprise. Preachers who simply raid the Bible for a clever idea-starter are failing to tap into the Spirit-powered message, and they are failing to appreciate the nature of divine revelation. Expository preaching is a necessary implication for those who affirm divine inspiration and authority of the biblical text. Since the Bible is God's specific self-revelation, preachers must manage it with exegetical integrity. Consequently, engaging expository preaching is the

---

[72] See Romans 10:9-17.
[73] 2 Corinthians 4:2.
[74] 2 Corinthians 4:7.

best and most effective form of gospel presentation. A preacher, therefore, is to be a herald of God who speaks forth the will of the Lord as presented in the Word of God. The preacher must always look to the Bible as the primary material for Christian truth proclamation.

Chapter 6
Exegesis, Exposition, and Application of the Text

With a high view of Scripture that affirms divine revelation and recognition of authority inherent in the text comes the need to engage seriously in the process of exegesis and exposition. Very simply put, exegesis is to identify the meaning from the text. Exposition is then the revealing of that meaning. Wayne McDill explains.

> The word exposition is from the Latin, *exposito*, meaning "a setting forth, narration, or display." As applied to preaching, the word has come to mean the setting forth or explanation of the message of the biblical text. In expository preaching the sermon is designed to communicate what the text says, including its meaning for the contemporary audience.[75]

Douglas Stuart, in his handbook for students and pastors on Old Testament exegesis, presents a "short guide" for sermon exegesis. It is intended "to provide the pastor with a handy format to follow in doing exegetical work on a passage of Scripture for the

---

[75] Wayne McDill. *12 Essential Skills for Great Preaching*, (Nashville: Broadman & Holman, 2006), 8.

purpose of preaching competently on it."[76] Here is the process Stuart suggests:

1. Text and Translation
   1.1 Read the passage repeatedly
   1.2 Check for significant textual issues
   1.3 Make your own translation
   1.4 Compile a list of alternatives
   1.5 Start a sermon use list
2. Literary-Historical Context
   2.1 Examine the background of the passage
   2.2 Describe the literary-historical setting
   2.3 Examine the foreground of the passage
3. Form and Structure
   3.1 Identify the genre and the form
   3.2 Investigate the life setting of forms where appropriate
   3.3 Look for structural patterns
   3.4 Isolate unique features and evaluate their significance
4. Grammatical and Lexical Data
   4.1 Note any grammar that is unusual, ambiguous, or otherwise important
   4.2 Make a list of the key terms
   4.3 Pare down the list to manageable size
   4.4 Do a mini word study of at least one word or term
5. Biblical and Theological Context
   5.1 Analyze use of the passage elsewhere in Scripture
   5.2 Analyze the passage's relation to the rest

---

[76]Douglas Stuart. *Old Testament Exegesis: A Handbook for Students and Pastors* (Louisville: Westminster / John Knox Press, 2001), 67. 3rd ed.

of Scripture
5.3 Analyze the passage's use in and relation to theology
6. Application
   6.1 List the life issues in the passage
   6.2 Clarify the possible nature and area of application
   6.3 Identify the audience and categories of application
   6.4 Establish the time focus and limits of the application
7. Moving from Exegesis to Sermon
   7.1 Work from your sermon use list
   7.2 Do not use the twelve – or six – step exegesis outline as the sermon outline
   7.3 Differentiate between the speculative and the certain
   7.4 Differentiate between the central and the peripheral
   7.5 Trust the homiletical commentaries only so far
   7.6 Remember that application is the ultimate concern of a sermon[77]

While Stuart's suggestions are helpful and thorough, the reality is preachers rarely go through this entire process. The solution is not to abandon the process altogether. Rather, the preacher should participate in exegetical engagement with the text in an

---

[77] Stuart, *Old Testament Exegesis*, 67-87. Gordon D. Fee, in his complementary handbook on New Testament exegesis, lays out a very similar procedure. Both texts serve as foundational instruction for integrating exegesis and homiletics.

ongoing manner to "fill himself" and "familiarize himself" so the process becomes more comfortable. It should be done to the degree that he begins to think routinely in an exegetical fashion. Consequently, the expository preacher matures to the point where he automatically goes through the process of checks and balances in his mind as he prepares sermons.

Walter Kaiser laments a "crisis in the pulpit" where "biblical exposition has become a lost art in contemporary preaching."[78] The remedy is a recovery of sound exegetical skills by the preacher. The preacher then uses these skills in his sermon construction routine. If the preacher claims a high view of Scripture that ascribes authority to the text, then he should back up his profession with the practice of serious engagement with the text.

However, expository preaching is more than good exegesis and exposition of the text. There must also be effective application. This aspect adds a component that requires the hearers to encounter and internalize the message presented. Hershael York says this:

> Our preaching must be lashed to the Scriptures. We are committed to think deeply and clearly about what the text means so we can also show

---

[78]Walter C. Kaiser Jr., *Toward An Exegetical Theology: Biblical Exegesis for Preaching & Teaching* (Grand Rapids: Baker Books, 1981), 36-37.

how it applies. Furthermore, we keep an eye on the audience as well so we can craft the sermon in such a way that takes into account the way our audience perceives. Everything we do is orchestrated to serve one goal: communicating what God has spoken in the most accurate and compelling way possible.[79]

Michael Quicke argues for what he calls transformational, incarnational, and diverse preaching. By transformational, he intends to convey preaching must be meaningful and result in something happening. Preaching is not just about postulating on potential, but should enact actual movement.[80] By incarnational, he means preaching should point to the "grand narrative"[81] of Jesus Christ as the story of the Word become flesh. Quicke is trying to make the point that there has never been one exclusive pattern for preaching, and in the modern age so often characterized by radical change, we should expect just as much diversity as we find in the New Testament.[82]

Quicke says, "Preaching's diversity in the New Testament, and ever since, makes it difficult to

---

[79] Hershael W. York, "Communication Theory and Text-Driven Preaching" in *Text-Driven Preaching: God' Word at the Heart of Every Sermon* (Nashville: B&H Academic, 2010), 232.
[80] Quicke, *360 Degree Preaching*, 23-24.
[81] Ibid, 25.
[82] Ibid, 26.

construct a single workable definition."[83] Nevertheless, he states his "conviction is that preaching is nothing less than sharing the in-breaking of God's good news to create new people in new community."[84] He points to the ministry of Christ to bolster this minimalist approach. He spotlights the fact that "when Jesus Christ came proclaiming (Mark 1:14), his primary concern was not to impart new information but to announce a new way of living in his kingdom."[85] He acknowledges "some may find this broad, dynamic definition of preaching unsatisfying," but goes forward in advocating expository preaching as a philosophy rather than a method.[86]

Donald Sunukjian offers a truncated model for sermon construction. He presents the idea that the preacher should first "look at what God is saying."[87] In this mode the preacher studies the passage and outlines the flow. Next, he must move from history to timeless truth and then form the take-home truth. The second component to his model is for the preacher to "look at what God is saying to us." [88] Here the preacher crafts his lesson and prepares to deliver it effectively.

---

[83]Ibid.
[84]Ibid, 27.
[85]Ibid.
[86]Ibid, 28.
[87]Donald R. Sunukjian. *Invitation to Biblical Preaching* (Grand Rapids: Kregel Pub., 2007), 9.
[88]Ibid, 87.

I have attempted to interact with helpful instruction from homiletic experts. However, each preacher must discover his own "pulpit identity" and "preaching voice." This only happens after much preaching. Preachers should be able to self-analyze their sermons and rightly classify their technique. Inability to do so evidences a haphazard approach to their pulpit time. Certainly, it is good that we have diversity in skill, personality, and technique. Different people in the pew respond better to some preachers and their style than others. However, I am asserting there is a core philosophical approach that should undergird and guide every preacher. All sermon construction and delivery should be rooted in the base operating system of the expository model. This is not a sterile, erudite exercise in academic elitism. Rather, the preacher begins in the place where God intends, His Word, and declares the truth for the sake of souls. Faithful preachers know where the starting point is: the text. When it is preached, people will respond.

The exegesis, exposition, and application of the text of Scripture are at the core of the preacher's job description. The Greek scholar A.T. Robertson wrote:

> We excuse other men for not having a technical knowledge of the Bible. But the preacher cannot be excused from an accurate apprehension of the

New Testament. This is the book that he undertakes to expound. It is his specialty.[89]

For expository preaching to happen, the preacher must develop the skill of exegesis. He must also hone his expositional ability. Finally, he must work to effectively apply the message to the listeners. This is to be the preacher's specialty.

Every preacher is an exegete to some degree. Launching into in-depth analysis of the text for sermon preparation should not be viewed as a burden or drudgery. If this is something you abhor then, perhaps, you should re-evaluate your commitment to preaching ministry. Exegetically unpacking the meaning of a text is a task preachers should gladly take up.

---

[89] A.T. Robertson, *The Minister and His Greek New Testament* (New York: George H. Doran Co., 1923), 20.

Chapter 7
A Suggested Sermon Delivery Model

Every preacher is unique and has different gifts and strengths. No model for sermon delivery fits everyone, and in fact, this is good. The church needs the diversity of preachers with their various areas of focus, perspectives, and talents.[90] However, it is my conviction every preacher should have the expository philosophy as an essential part of his preaching repertoire.[91]

Expository preaching is a necessary implication for those who affirm divine revelation and authority of the biblical text. If the Bible is truly from God Almighty, it demands to be proclaimed expositionally. The sequence is this: divinely inspired revelation implies inherent authority implies careful management / interpretation implies expository preaching that includes application.

A major goal in the life of the church is that her people be careful readers of the text. The people in the

---

[90]For a defense of topical preaching see Erwin W. Lutzer's article "A Response to Homiletics and Hermeneutics" in *Hermeneutics, Inerrancy, and the Bible*. Ed. Earl D. Radmacher and Robert D. Preus (Grand Rapids: Zondervan, 1984), 833-387.

[91]Walter C. Kaiser Jr.'s text *Toward an Exegetical Theology* is, in my opinion, vital reading material for those who would preach expositionally. Chapter one of that text titled "Current Crises in Exegetical Theology" is worth the price of the book.

pew will handle the Bible the way they see it modeled in the pulpit. If it is managed cavalierly by the preacher it will be treated sloppily by the Christian. Instead, the preacher should profess his respect for Scripture and back it up by preaching it with care.

He must also couple care with a delivery that meaningfully tries to connect with the hearers. My homiletics teacher and doctoral faculty supervisor, Dr. Hershael York, went to great effort to drive home what he felt was a key principle for us preachers: "Don't be boring!" Thus, he advocated *engaging* exposition. This is not outlandish showmanship. Rather, it is the legitimate expression of passion in the pulpit that cannot help but activate interest in the pew.

In preaching, the homilitician attempts a triple engagement. First, he must himself engage with the text. Then, he must engage with the audience. Finally, he works to engage the audience with the text. While there are many techniques for trying to accomplish this merging, I want to offer a concise approach.

Abundant resources are available for learning the expository method, but here I simply want to suggest a basic model for sermon delivery. This is a model I have adopted. While I do not preach this way all the time, I have tried to make it my default homiletic. It is intentionally succinct, focusing on the irreducible parts.

A Suggested Sermon Delivery Model

1. **Reading a logical block of biblical text.** The sermon text is most often a paragraph, occasionally a verse or two, and sometimes an entire chapter. I like to begin with the reading of the sermon text because it strikes an appropriate tone when read with conviction. It encourages the hearers to focus on God's Word and it establishes where primary attention is to be. We want to be careful readers of the text.

2. **An engaging verbal illustration.** An applicable contemporary-life connection should be made with the audience. The illustration should be concisely worded and emotionally effective. I believe a single quality illustration that is well developed and dynamically presented is better than multiple mini illustrations that make small points, though both are useful. Preferably an *inclusio* illustration is best, one you return to at the end of the sermon, but with an added idea-advancing component.[92]

3. **Expositional movement through the text.** This textual engagement should include some degree of

---

[92]For a brief mention of this idea see Grant Osborne, *The Hermeneutical Spiral*, 54.

the historical and literary context of the passage, its subject matter, and meaning. This is not to be a running commentary, but rather an engaging unfolding of the biblical narrative. This is the teaching meat of the sermon, where the preacher's time in expositional study bears fruit. It is good for the preacher to make intermittent application to the audience during this movement.

4. **A single big idea emphasis.** I have discovered postmoderns will typically not remember multiple points. I readily admit exceptions to this. Nevertheless, I favor a single "big idea" philosophy that seeks to emphasize the main meaning of the passage. The main point of the sermon will be derived from the main point of the text. I often present this main lesson from a variety of applicational angles to reinforce it in the hearts of the hearers.

5. **Thoughtful conclusion.** Spend time crafting your conclusion. Too often preachers simply allow the conclusion to happen without any planning. Engineer your conclusions intentionally. It is my opinion, perhaps misguided, that conclusions should stop the sermon. Do not mislead the audience into thinking you are done when you

really intend to preach for ten more minutes.

A preacher needs only spend a few minutes in the "preaching" section of a Christian bookstore to realize a host of sermon delivery models and suggestions are readily available. I certainly do not claim this to be the "end all" method. Rather, this is offered simply as *a* model, not *the* model, for expository sermon delivery. Varieties of style are beneficial in the church and my hope is this approach will complement preachers' philosophy of sermon matriculation. My prayer is this will function for some as a helpful model as they "preach the word."[93]

---

[93]2 Timothy 4:2.

Chapter 8
The Gospel Must Be Communicated and a Response is Required

Preaching has a specific purpose: to promote faith development. The Apostle Paul lays out the process in Romans 10:9-17 with an advancing wave of movement culminating with this statement: "So faith comes from hearing, and hearing through the word of Christ." Gospel proclamation is a vehicle for faith. Preaching is designed to convey God's message of redemption to humanity. Therefore, preaching is intended to proclaim the truth of the gospel message and encourage hearers to respond to its call.

The result is redemptive gospel preaching. This type of proclamation means we place emphasis on the gospel and declare "repentance toward God and of faith in our Lord Jesus Christ."[94] Hence, "we proclaim Him."[95] The not-so-hidden agenda of Christian preaching is to bring lost sinners into a right relationship with God by means of the cross of Christ. The gospel, "good news," of Jesus Christ is the power of God to save humanity.[96] That message is to be powerfully declared in our churches. Thus, the supreme

---

[94] See Acts 20:21 and its context.
[95] Note Colossians 1:28-29.
[96] See Romans 1:16 and its context.

implication of true Christian preaching is that it draws people to God. The German theologian Deitrich Bonhoeffer wrote, "A truly evangelical sermon must be like offering a child a beautiful red apple or holding out a glass of water to a thirsty man and asking 'Wouldn't you like it?'"[97] The goal of expository preaching is to allow the Holy Spirit to convict the hearers by the message preached so they may repent and respond to God's offer of forgiveness and grace through the blood of Christ.[98] Preaching puts the love of God on display, and the love of God is manifest best at the cross of Christ. Hence, preaching pulls people to the cross and dramatically shows them their Savior.

Friendship evangelism is fine unless it's all friendship and no evangelism. In fact, evangelism does not happen until the gospel is spoken. We may lay the groundwork through relationship building and rapport development, but those things are to lead to the specific message of Jesus Christ. Evangelistic preaching always calls for hearers to respond appropriately to God's grace and offer of redemption. Whether they choose to respond is ultimately between them and God, but the preacher is to be faithful in the teaching and telling. Martin Luther is cited as saying, "The first

---

[97]Dietrich Bonhoeffer, *Worldly Preaching*, ed. Clyde E. Fant (New York: Thomas Nelson, 1975), 16.
[98]See Ephesians 2:8,9 and its context.

duty of the gospel preacher is to declare God's law and to show the nature of sin."

We should also be concerned with teaching the simplicity of the gospel. Do not over-complicate the message of the cross by peppering it with speculative theological theories. Certainly, the preacher should think theologically and wrestle with complex doctrines. But he should not allow his lofty opinions to quagmire evangelistic movement. Giving advice to preachers, C.H. Spurgeon, wanted to emphasize the missional aspect of preaching. He said this: "To win a soul from going down into the pit is a more glorious achievement than to be crowned in the arena of theological controversy as Doctor Sufficientissimus; to have faithfully unveiled the glory of God in the face of Jesus Christ will be in the final judgment accounted worthier service than to have solved the problems of the religious Sphinx, or to have cut the Gordian knot of Apocalyptic difficulty."[99] Remember, preaching is primarily about presenting God's Word, which then works to convict sinners to repent and be saved. It is the powerful gospel that saves not the theologian's IQ.

Preaching should include the correct information about what a person must do to be saved. The gospel is the "good news" about God's nature of love, mercy,

---

[99] C.H. Spurgeon, *Lectures to My Students* (Grand Rapids: Zondervan, 1954), 80.

and grace. He refused to leave us in our sin and thus sent his Son to serve, heal, teach, and die for us. Jesus, the Son of God, became a human man, yet retained his divine personhood, so that he could be the necessary atoning sacrifice to reconcile us to God. We locate our Christian identity at the cross of Christ. Jesus was crucified and buried, but rose that early Sunday morning, pioneering the path for our eternity.

The gospel message not only involves what has been done on our behalf by God in the past. It also presents a required human response. To be saved, we must first understand we are condemned by our sin and in need of a savior.[100] Thankfully, God, through the atoning sacrifice of Jesus Christ on the cross, has made provision for our forgiveness and freedom from sin. To access this provision we must first learn and engage with the gospel message that, through Christ, we can have eternal life.[101] We must have faith Jesus is who he claimed to be, the Son of God and redeemer of humanity.[102] We must be willing to repent or turn from a former life of sin and commit to the Christian faith.[103] We must confess/affirm/admit our belief that Jesus Christ is the son of God.[104] Next, we must be

---

[100]Romans 3:23.
[101]John 3:16; 14:6.
[102]Romans 10:17; Ephesians 2:8,9; Hebrews 11:6.
[103]Luke 13:3.
[104]Matthew 10:32.

baptized/immersed in water for the forgiveness of sins.[105] Baptism is the culminating component to the conversion event, but it is not the end. Rather, baptism marks the beginning of new life in Christ.[106] We are added to the church and henceforth seek to live a faithful and devoted life for God's glory.

So, the gospel is about God's love, Jesus' sacrifice, and our submissive obedient faith. However, there is also to be ongoing gospel living. The church is constituted by Christians in the community of faith who are living transformed lives. The gospel changes people and gives fresh priorities and practices for how we live in this world. It is this gospel agenda that the expository preacher promotes.

An additional word of caution is necessary. The preacher must take care not to alter the gospel. We don't smother seekers with the gospel but we must present it with honesty, resisting the temptation to smooth its rough edges. Preachers face powerful cultural pressure to sweep hard issues under the rug but the message of the cross refuses to be sanitized. Also, since the power of God to save is coupled with the gospel, the preacher risks divesting the gospel of its salvific effectiveness by changing the message. Acknowledgment of this unalterable message is a

---

[105] Acts 2:38; 22:16; Galatians 3:27.
[106] Romans 6:3-11.

component of the expository preaching philosophy. Preachers must honor fidelity to the gospel message because it is the gospel that saves. Again, it is God through the gospel who transforms lives, not the preacher himself.

Authentic and effective evangelistic preaching is only accomplished when the Bible-pictured gospel is taught. Some may argue, "Why all this fuss about the Bible? Why not just preach Jesus?" My response would be this: "Okay, which Jesus do you want to preach because there are many pictured?" Only the picture of Jesus presented by an inerrant Bible matters. Our preaching of Jesus can only follow when we have first seriously engaged him in the Word. Remember, we, like Paul, are to preach the "whole council of God,"[107] and this implies the effectiveness, inerrancy, and all-sufficiency of Scripture.

Having stressed the need to be text driven, we also must remember that indeed the Bible has a main motif. The meta-narrative of Scripture is the Christ. Preachers need a healthy and balanced biblical theology approach to interpretation that accounts for the dynamic movement of the revealed text through time. The implication, therefore, is that the theme of ecclesial

---

[107]See Acts 20:27 and its context.

preaching ministry is Christ-centeredness.[108] This Christocentric hermeneutic, when applied to the enterprise of expository preaching, would first say Jesus is layered within the meta-narrative of every biblical context. Second, for the Christian preacher, Jesus is prominent in the application phase of interpretation and exposition.

The core claim of this hermeneutic is that preachers should have a Christocentric view of homiletics. Jesus Christ is the center of Scripture and should be at the center of the expository preaching philosophy. Hence, we place a spotlight on Jesus in our sermons. This includes the gospel, and the gospel message always calls for obedience.

On his post-resurrection walk with some disciples on the way to Emmaus, Jesus teaches "beginning with Moses and all the prophets, he interpreted to them the things written about himself in all the scriptures."[109] In his final appearance before his ascension, he said, "These are my words that I spoke to you while I was still with you, that everything written about me in the law of Moses and the prophets and the psalms must be

---

[108] The topic of Christ-centered preaching is much debated. There is ongoing conversation concerning the degree to which we locate Christ in every passage. Some who are currently engaged in this include: Sidney Gredanius, Graeme Goldsworthy, Walt Kaiser, Bryan Chapell, and Dennis Johnson.
[109] Luke 24:27.

fulfilled."[110] At that moment, Jesus "opened their minds so they could understand the scriptures."[111] The preaching enterprise endeavors to open minds to the centrality of Christ in all of Scripture.

This sentiment is what we could call "perspectival reading." Today's believers are "in-the-know" readers of the text because we see the Bible from the post-cross side of the historical-redemptive working of God. Thus, as insiders, we read and preach with a view to Jesus. We see Christ as the meta-narrative, the overall motif, but we also preach with micro-narrative insight. By "micro-narrative" I mean especially in the gospel accounts, we have access to details of Jesus' life. We do not have to preach him as a far off savior in the sky; we can preach intimate details of his life and ministry. Interestingly, so many of the gospel accounts detail his time spent in personal interaction with often unnamed people. This is very telling, and preachers should pick up on the obvious significance of these details.

The gospel accounts are biographies rooted in the narrative of biblical history. Expository preaching wonderfully tasks the preacher to access this narrative and tell the story of Jesus with more detail. Preachers should utilize the gospel accounts as micro-narrative. After all, history is perspectival; and when it comes to

---

[110]Luke 24:44.
[111]Luke 24:45.

the biography of Jesus, we have four perspectives. This is not an embarrassment for us, but an advantage.

Unfortunately, warnings of taking this perspective to an extreme should be well noted. We are cautioned, while Christ is the overarching theme, to press the matter of Christ-focus to every word of the canon is exegetically unwarranted. Furthermore, the danger in pressing this concept to every word of text is that it may easily descend into unhealthy allegorizing and overly imaginative typology. Is Christ the core meaning of the Bible? Yes. Is he explicitly the subject in every phrase? Probably not. While I find the broad version of a Christ-centered hermeneutic compelling, I am not completely sold on its exegetical/hermeneutical validity and am concerned with where it could lead. If it minimizes obedience to the entirety of Scripture then the hermeneutic has gone awry. If it promotes a greater appreciation for the atoning work of Jesus at the cross then it has functioned properly.

The Bible has multiple genres and angles of instruction; this is testimony to God's wisdom. The preacher should honor them all in his preaching ministry and resist the urge to force a narrow hermeneutic that fails to account for the Bible's cohesive complexity. Hence, biblical preaching requires checks and balances. The preacher weaves together healthy hermeneutics, honest exegesis, and homiletic expertise to preach Christ faithfully.

Preachers are correct to appeal to Christological meta-narrative. We preach "Jesus Christ and him crucified." Expositors are to look under the surface of the subject matter of the narrative and locate Christ as the real meaning of the text. A mediated hermeneutic that hinges on accepting the overarching principle of Christ as the center of God's revelation to the world leads to a sermon development style that consistently spotlights Jesus in the congregational setting and authentically drives listeners to gospel obedience. This focus must be balanced by even-keeled historical-literary exegesis. Yes, it's a good effort but must be hedged by correct hermeneutics. The Bible must be preached in all its fullness. Nevertheless, preachers should want the church to put on their Jesus-colored glasses and read the Bible with an ultimate view to the gospel of Christ.

In summary, the mission of expository preaching is to convey the saving gospel of Jesus Christ and call for a response. Also, the preaching of God's Word is for the up-building, maturing, and faith development of the church. Christians have heard the gospel but need to keep hearing it. After all, we are quite forgetful. Sermons should be planned for the overarching purpose of enhancing faith in the hearers. This should be the specific aim of expository preaching. Preaching calls for unbelievers to believe and believers to believe more. On these two objectives hang the whole of the preaching purpose.

Chapter 9
The Present Need for Expository Preaching

Preachers must not think the need for expository preaching is self-evident. Rather, its place in Christian ministry must be repeatedly advanced. Many church members need to be convinced of the validity and necessity of the approach. Furthermore, because the world today is saturated with distractions, the need for expository preaching is dire. The church must appreciate good expository preaching. Modern media conventions and the "busyness of life" have wreaked havoc on churches by destroying many churchgoers' interest in listening to the preaching of the Word of God. Today preachers are tasked with holding the fickle attention of the people in the pew and simultaneously connecting them with the message of Scripture. Part of the answer to this dilemma is more passion from the pulpit. John Broadus eloquently stated this:

> When a man who is apt in teaching, whose soul is on fire with the truth which he trusts has saved him and hopes will save others, speaks to his fellow-men, face to face, eye to eye, and electric sympathies flash to and fro between him and his hearers, till they lift each other up, higher and higher, into the intensest thought, and the most impassioned emotion—higher and yet higher, till

they are borne as on chariots of fire above the world-there is a power to move men, to influence character, life, destiny, such as no printed page, radio cabinet, or silver screen can ever possess.[112]

Many today view the Bible as an archaic and dead document, unworthy of time and attention. However, a preacher who cherishes exposition of the Word and has a well-developed philosophy of expository preaching that affirms divine special revelation, will understand the Bible is a living and timeless message that is eminently relevant to people's lives. The Word of God is still living and active.[113] It is alive with meaning and contains a redemptive message the world needs to hear. Therefore, the preacher must know the Word of God, know people, and know how to bring the two together.

For preaching to be effective in the church context, the preacher must himself be authentic. He must not do disservice to the Word by wedding it to a proclaimer with poor character. He must believe and live what he preaches. Also, the preaching event should be held in high esteem by the congregation. If the church thinks lowly of preaching then appreciation for the proclamation of the Word of God must be revived.

---

[112]John A. Broadus, *On the Preparation and Delivery of Sermons*. Rev. ed. (New York: Harper & Row Pub., 1944), 3.

[113]See Hebrews 4:12 and its context.

While Scripture itself is intrinsically relevant, the congregation must do its part in seeking the significance of the message for their lives. Furthermore, in the worship context, the preacher needs to exercise "engaging exposition." Expository preaching of the Word of God does not mean dry commentary or mere description of a biblical account. Rather, the preacher has his main "big idea" grounded and supported from the biblical text, but crafts the message in a way that utilizes illustrations and makes meaningful application. The expository sermon should engage the audience in a way that successfully connects them, where they are, to the timeless truths of Scripture.

This approach to sermon construction and delivery stresses the value of digging into the text beyond a mere surface-level engagement. Preachers are tasked with effectively exposing the complexity of the Bible. Yes, the gospel is simple, but it is not simplistic. There are rich layers and contours of meaning in the biblical text that the preacher, from the pulpit, should unfold. This declaration of the "manifold wisdom of God"[114] is what the world urgently requires. We need preachers who accept the duty of faithfully declaring God's truth.

I have heard many sermons that I call "information dumps." These sermons usually have many points and rapidly reference numerous Bible

---

[114] See Ephesians 3:10 and its context.

verses. I believe sermons should be grounded in Scripture, but gratuitous use of Bible references that butcher contexts is unhelpful. The expository sermon has one text block the preacher focuses on developing. Other passages may be used, but only when they legitimately advance the point and with fair contextual treatment. A sermon that dumps excessive information on the modern listener is usually quickly forgotten.

Furthermore, the expository approach to sermon construction and delivery addresses the need for doctrinal preaching. Doctrinal fidelity is a good thing, despite some dissenting opinions, and expository preaching allows for those issues to be brought up "organically." We don't have to artificially generate occasions to deal with doctrinal matters. Instead, as movement is made through a passage, those issues invariably arise from the text and can be readily discussed. Preachers should be sensitive to doctrinal issues in the text. They should identify and handle these issues with careful application to today's church. Indeed, we seek to model after the New Testament church pattern, but we should remember we are the church of today. Contemporary Christians need to be convinced of the value of generational doctrinal fidelity. Preaching is a vehicle to ensure the preservation of the faith among the saints.

Permit me also to mention briefly the role of emotion in the sermon. God created us with both intellectual and emotional capacities. Preachers should address both. Often preachers are leery of making any kind of emotional appeal due to perceived abuses by so many. However, a remonstrance toward an abuse does not negate the legitimacy of the approach.

A faithful leader in the Lord's church once told me about his emotional conversion journey. He had studied the gospel and had attended church for some time, but had never made his commitment to Christ in baptism. In fact, he did not believe he needed to confess Christ or be baptized until the preacher delivered an expository sermon on the fifth chapter of Second Kings concerning the healing of Naaman's leprosy. The text was preached with richness and detail. However, it was also delivered with passion and struck an emotional cord. He felt a profound emotional connection with Naaman, and that connection is what finally prompted him to realize his arrogance in rejecting baptism. God used an expository sermon that included passionate emotional appeal to accomplish his work of saving.

The authentic expository preacher has a passion for the text that is bound to outflow. His emotional connection with the text models for listeners the relationship they, too, can have with God's Word.

Expository preaching has power to move hearts because it taps into the divine power outlet: Scripture. The Bible is infused with otherworldly power because it was divinely crafted and delivered through inspiration. Expository preaching is Holy Spirit-driven preaching. When we affirm the Spirit's role in revealing truth through the Word, we recognize a nature to the text wherein even the details are important. Often the way points are sequentially developed in the text bear the earmarks of the Spirit's wisdom. Who are we to tamper with, raid, and butcher the contexts of Scriptures the Holy Spirit perfectly delivered? Let's instead preach them the way that best honors Him: expositionally in context.

When the preacher truly believes preaching echoes the truths of God, he will be infused with respect for the preaching task. The man in the pulpit will be filled with awe for God that then migrates to the people in the pew. The expository preaching perspective offers a helpful homiletic cognizance. The preacher remembers there is power within his biblical sermon to change lives.

Expository preaching is a spiritual enterprise needed today and always. In many churches it has become a lost art and needs to be recovered. A commitment to the expository model of preaching is a necessary implication of a high view of Scripture. We pray the Lord will raise up diligent proclaimers of His Word who deeply affirm the worth of the text and preach it accordingly.

Chapter 10
Conclusion

God has spoken and we hang on his every word. After all, "Man shall not live by bread alone, but by every word that comes from the mouth of God."[115] The Bible is God's self-disclosure of his identity and will. Hence, the Christian preacher is called to "preach the word." To engage faithfully in the enterprise of expository preaching he starts by affirming divine revelation. This principle implies real authority in the text. Then, with a healthy understanding of inspiration, he is equipped to engage the text. Next, the preacher takes on the role of exegete as he seeks authorial intent. Preaching is the exposition and application of the biblical text and acts as a means to connect people with the Word of God. The concept of expository preaching is the best homiletic model because it connects people with God through the vehicle of Scripture.

Jesus Christ constitutes the core of what the preacher declares. We preach Christ. Furthermore, the preaching event should be done with "engaging exposition" that meaningfully reaches the listeners through sound technique and effective delivery. The result is application. The listeners understand what they hear preached. They internalize the message and seek

---

[115] Matthew 4:4 with Deuteronomy 8:3 as its antecedent.

to apply it to their lives. The consequence is a response of repentance resulting in redemption. Effective preaching accesses the Word of God and gives it opportunity to foster submissive obedient faith in the lives of listeners. The goal is for people to be closer to God and conform more and more to the image of Jesus Christ.

Sundays do not stop coming. I once heard a preacher say "Preaching is like giving birth on Sunday and waking up Monday realizing you are pregnant again!" It is a daunting task to stand and speak for God. It is a glorious yet imminently humbling work. The expository preacher puts his trust in God and steps into the pulpit with something meaningful to say. It is deemed meaningful not because it is the product of his cleverness or oratory ingenuity, but because he has filled himself with God's Word through exegetical engagement and is proclaiming divine truth.

I am convinced Christians do not hate expository preaching. They hate *poor* expository preaching. Whether they know it or not, the church desperately needs excellent preaching. So preachers -stop goofing off. Let's step up to the challenge and faithfully participate in the legacy of declaring the Word for the glory of God.

Appendix 1 – Verbal Illustrations and Devotionals

Identifying effective verbal illustrations for the message can be the most time consuming part of sermon construction. There is no shortage of lame illustrations, but meaningful and engaging expository preaching requires dynamic illustrations that promote application. I encourage preachers to be discerning about their verbal illustrations. It is pandering, not preaching, when we tell a laugh-evoking joke in a sermon that has no connection to the text. Granted, the utilization of illustrations is a judgment call that should correspond to the diverse preaching styles. Hence, it is impossible to issue hard and fast rules about which illustrations are "good" and "bad." But remember, the text –not the illustration– should drive the sermon. Illustrations are simply homiletic tools that assist in linking hearers to the real substance of the sermon: the biblical text.

With that in mind, I offer the following assortment of fifteen brief articles. They include various descriptive illustrations, basic devotional thoughts, and short exegetical examples of handling a text. These are articles I wrote mostly for church bulletins. My hope is that they will serve as a sampling of various illustrative techniques. Some of them focus on a text that they then attempt to engagingly develop. Others key in on a vivid mental picture and attempt to emotionally and intellectually connect with the listeners. The pedagogy is impeded because they are in written form, which is very different from the oratory presentation. Nevertheless, my hope is they will be of some benefit as you think about crafting your illustrations and describing your texts for preaching.

Devotional Thought 1
Ten Thousand Angels

"For our sake he made him to be sin who knew no sin, so that in him we might become the righteousness of God."

(2 Corinthians 5:21)

When I was a kid, my favorite church song was "Ten Thousand Angels." As a young boy, I was enamored with the idea of God's well-armed angelic army. I could imagine them sweeping upon the earth to destroy those tyrants who were arresting and crucifying Jesus. For me, it roused this aggressive idea of God using military force to accomplish his will, springing into action with a celestial rescue mission while killing the bad guys.

Thankfully, God has accomplished his will without requiring our destruction. Though, because of our sin, we deserved no pardon, he, nevertheless, poured out his mercy and grace for our forgiveness in the death of his son (Romans 5:15-21). In fact, the death of Jesus on the cross was the key part of God's redemptive plan for humanity's atonement (1 Peter 2:24; 3:18; Philippians 2:8; Colossians 2:13-14).

Even now, I can vividly imagine as Jesus was being arrested, mistreated, and crucified, the armies of heaven were watching with disgust. I envisage legions of angels with swords drawn, grimaces on their faces, on the edge of heaven just longing for the "go" signal to descend and make right with supernatural force the terrible injustice they were seeing. I imagine this powerful army was leaning off the brink of heaven's edge on their tiptoes just itching to crash down upon wicked humanity and rescue Jesus Christ from the villains. I can hear them muttering through gritted teeth, "He belongs on the throne of heaven and not on a human cross of shame."

And then I imagine my Lord Jesus Christ giving them a gentle "no" nod and speaking these words: "Put your sword back into its place. Do you think that I cannot appeal to my Father, and he will at once send me more than twelve legions of angels? But how then should the Scriptures be fulfilled, that it must be so?" (Matthew 26:52-54).

Jesus remained faithful to the divine plan of our redemption that included his death, even though that involved horrible suffering and sacrifice on his part. He endured the cross because, for us to have eternal life, "it must be so."

You see, it was not really the soldiers who held Jesus captive. He didn't need angels to come and rescue him. Rather, he was compelled to submit to those sinful men because of his love for us. He endured the humiliation for us. Though they struck him and they cursed him and mocked his holy name, he suffered everything for you and me.

Devotional Thought 2
The Secret of the Easy Yoke

"Come to me, all who labor and are heavy laden, and I will give you rest. Take my yoke upon you, and learn from me, for I am gentle and lowly in heart, and you will find rest for your souls. For my yoke is easy, and my burden is light."
(Matthew 11:28-30)

In Matthew 11:28-30 Jesus offers much needed rest to weary sinners. He says, "Come to me, all who labor and are heavy laden, and I will give you rest." This is certainly a comforting invitation. However, he then has the audacity to call for us to take his yoke upon us. What a seeming contradiction! Since when does a yoke mean rest? Sounds like work to me. Nevertheless, Jesus said, "Take my yoke upon you, and learn from me, for I am gentle and lowly in heart, and you will find rest for your souls. For my yoke is easy, and my burden is light."

In this passage, Jesus is teaching something that takes us a long time to figure out. He's telling us, while we delight in the relationship of grace we as believers experience in Christ, the relationship characterized by spiritual peace and the promise of eternal rest, there is another necessary component to Christianity:

obedience. God has not given us strict commands because he is cruel, but to establish boundaries for our ultimate good. In our lives, we must strive to properly balance duty and delight, obedience and relationship.

Here's the secret of the easy yoke: Acquire a taste for obedience. The burden is light when we are in a spiritually mature state that understands the purposes of obedience and delights in doing things God's way. This comes only after a lifestyle of submission to the Lord has been cultivated. That's the secret. We have learned through time and experience to appreciate and delight in God's commands. We arrived at this sanctified state by consistently following his will. Hence, we obey not with a grudge but with gladness and joy (Deuteronomy 28:46).

Devotional Thought 3
Racing through Hebrews 12

"Consider him who endured from sinners such hostility against himself, so that you may not grow weary or fainthearted."
(Hebrews 12:3)

Hebrews 12 is an elegant presentation of the believers' confidence in Christ. The writer employs persuasive appeal to convict us in our resolve to stay true to Jesus.

It begins with a climactic summary of faith's journey that challenges believers to "lay aside every weight, and sin which clings so closely" (vs. 1b). Setting aside sin means we can then "run with endurance the race that is set before us" (vs.1c). This race of faith is only successful when we are "looking to Jesus, the founder and perfector of our faith" (vs. 2a).

Consequently, we are to "consider him" (vs. 3a). This declaration yanks our attention away from the trivial and calls us to let Jesus capture our full focus. This fixation of faith's gaze upon Christ ensures that "we may not grow weary or fainthearted" (vs. 3b).

The reader is reminded of the solemn scene when ancient Israel is gathered at Mount Sinai to codify their covenant with God (Hebrews 12:18-21; Exodus 19:1-

20:21). There was thunder and lightning, a thick cloud of smoke over the mount, and the sound of trumpet blasts. The earth shook. No one could touch the mountain or they would perish, and God's voice crashed upon the assembly with terrifying effect.

The writer of Hebrews contrasts the inauguration of the Sinai covenant at the mountain event with the "new covenant" (vs. 24). With compounding emphasis, he points us beyond Sinai to Zion: "But you have come to Mount Zion and to the city of the living God, the heavenly Jerusalem, and to innumerable angels in festal gathering, and to the assembly of the firstborn who are enrolled in heaven, and to God the judge of all, and to the spirits of the righteous made perfect" (vs. 22-23). The haymaker point comes to its apex as he says, "And to Jesus, the mediator of a new covenant, and to the sprinkling blood that speaks a better word than the blood of Abel" (vs. 24). The blood of Abel speaks a word of vengeance, but the blood of Christ is a better word of forgiveness.

This point heightens our appreciation of what we are a part of. In the church of Christ, we are participants in a majestic covenant event. We're part of something superior to all previous relationship contracts. Being a blood-bought, baptized believer entails unimaginable privileges, yet also serious responsibilities. Because Christians are honored to be part of the "kingdom that cannot be shaken" (vs. 28a); "thus let us offer to God acceptable worship, with reverence and awe" (vs. 28b). And don't forget the sobering reality that "our God is a consuming fire" (vs. 29).

These twenty-nine verses of Hebrews 12 teach us Jesus is the founder and completer of our faith. Because we persist in looking to him, we do not grow weary in being devoted. We are participants in a glorious kingdom that cannot be shaken, and our response is one of gratitude and worship. May we, as the church, ever hold to our confidence in Christ with true faithfulness.

Devotional Thought 4
Let the Word Speak

"Therefore we must pay much closer attention to what we have heard, lest we drift away from it." (Hebrews 2:1)

In preaching, the power is always in the Word. It's not about the eloquence or charisma of the speaker. It's about God molding us for eternity through the proclamation of Scripture (1 Corinthians 1:21; Romans 10:13-17). The preaching of God's Word is a serious task for me as the preacher, but also for you as the listener. It is a time when we quiet our spirit and let the Holy Spirit talk. Whenever we hear the Bible preached, we must let the Word speak to us and change us into someone who looks more and more like Jesus.

From time to time, it's good to reflect on where we've been and what's ahead. Currently, we are in the midst of a series from the New Testament book of Hebrews. But it's not just a sermon series from me. You are involved in the process. What we discuss together in the Wednesday night auditorium class finds its way into the sermon the following Sunday. Our Bible study is always based on the text that will be preached at the following Sunday worship service. Doing this provides continuity in what is taught, discussed, preached, reviewed, and applied.

The interpretation of Scripture is the work of the whole church. Therefore, we go about this serious work of engagement with the text together. The upcoming sermons will be based on the last half of the book of Hebrews. I invite you to engage eagerly in the preaching event as we leap into Scripture together. The over-arching goal of our study in the book of Hebrews is to better know Jesus. What a wonderful use of our time and concentration!

Please pray for me as I preach God's Word. And pray for the hearts of the listeners, that they might be moved -not by my "style" or "delivery technique," but by the holy Word of God, which is able to prick the soul and draw people near to God. Let the Word speak.

Devotional Thought 5
God Doesn't Wear Out

> "Of old you laid the foundation of the earth,
> and the heavens are the work of your hands.
> They will perish, but you will remain; they will all
> wear out like a garment. You will change them
> like a robe, and they will pass away, but you are the
> same, and your years have no end."
> (Psalm 102:25-27)

Do you ever feel worn out? In Hebrews 1:10-12, the writer draws from Psalm 102:25-27 to highlight the reality that God is all-powerful and everlasting. Though the world wears out, the Lord remains forever. Amazingly, the author is connecting the power of God with the nature of the Son. Jesus Christ is the agency of creation itself, and that role rightly entitles him to divine privilege. That means all humanity is under the authority of Jesus. Nothing and no one is higher in supremacy than him. Christ is incomparably great. The superiority of the Christian faith is grounded on the lordship of Jesus.

In your moments of spiritual exhaustion, lean on Jesus. He is the sustainer of the universe, and he can hold you up. Jesus never goes out of date. He never gets old and fragile. He never feels exhausted from being too busy. He is strong enough to bear your burdens. When you feel worn out think about Jesus. Think about his ability to constantly empower you for faith. It's not just about what he did for us in the past on the cross. It's also about what he continues to do each day in the lives of believers. You can trust his sustaining power for your soul because he doesn't wear out.

Devotional Thought 6
When You're at the End of Your Rope

"And the woman said to Elijah, 'Now I know that you are a man of God, and that the word of the LORD in your mouth is truth.' "
(1 Kings 17:24)

What do you do when you're at the end of your rope? We've heard it said, "You tie a knot and hang on." But, as Christians, we have more to hang onto than just a rope. Because we worship a God who has demonstrated the power of resurrection through his own Son, who was raised on the third day after he was crucified, we know he has indeed given us the truth we need to live our lives.

In 1 Kings 17:8-24, we read of a very desperate situation. The prophet Elijah is in hiding because of a decree by the evil King Ahab and his wife Jezebel sentencing him to death. God instructs Elijah to go and stay with a poor widow and her son who live in Zarephath. Although God makes miraculous provision for them to avoid starvation, things go from bad to worse when the widow's son dies. They are brought to a breaking point, and the widow of Zarephath lashes out at the prophet of God.

However, when we are at the end of our rope, God can bring new life to our desperate situation. With the raising to life of the widow's dead child, the Lord demonstrated He is the source of life and truth. This biblical narrative teaches us Christians have more to hang onto than a rope. We have the powerful promises of an almighty God who assures us all things will work out for ultimate good.

Devotional Thought 7
Unity in the Church

"I appeal to you, brothers, by the name of our Lord Jesus Christ, that all of you agree and that there be no divisions among you, but that you be united in the same mind and the same judgment."
(1 Corinthians 1:10)

Two porcupines found themselves in a blizzard and tried to huddle together to keep warm. But because they were pricked by each other's quills, they moved apart. Soon they were shivering again and had to lay side by side once more for their own survival. They needed each other, even though they needled each other.

So it is in the church. We each have our own perspectives and opinions, and they sometimes collide with other perspectives and opinions. Furthermore, we each have our foibles and bad attitudes. Put us all together in the church, and conflict and communication difficulties often develop. However, as fellow believers in this community of faith, we must forgive one another and accommodate one another's opinions. In matters that are essentials of faith, there must be unity and agreement (1 Corinthians 1:10). However, in matters of opinion, there must be leeway, liberty, accommodation, and patience.

Consider these four simple, practical things you can do to promote unity in the church. First, pray. This is what Jesus did (John 17:20-23). Second, cultivate an attitude of peace. Matthew 5:9 says, "Blessed are the peacemakers" not "Blessed are the troublemakers." Third, demonstrate your love for the brethren. Don't fail to back up your claims of care and concern with authentic actions of love (John 13:35). Fourth, acquire the skill of healthy communication.

Christians are to experience a bond with one another that unites them in common fellowship and oneness. God did not design us to live out our faith in isolation. Rather, he designed the church to function as a community of believers. Within this community, we work to foster fellowship and unity that provide great opportunities to build stronger ties with fellow Christians and to experience mutual encouragement. Let there be unity in the church.

Devotional Thought 8
Find Out Where the Road Takes You

> "And beginning with Moses and all the Prophets, he interpreted to them in all the Scriptures the things concerning himself."
>
> (Luke 24:27)

On the day Jesus was resurrected from the grave, two disciples were traveling down a road on their way home to Emmaus. As they walked, a stranger joined them on the journey. The three began to talk together about the recent news, and the two travelers expressed their discouragement to the stranger over what had just happened in Jerusalem regarding the death of Christ. They told the stranger they'd hoped Jesus was the one who would redeem Israel. The stranger interrupted them and said, "O foolish ones, and slow of heart to believe all that the prophets have spoken! Was it not necessary that the Christ should suffer these things and enter into his glory?" (Luke 24:26). He then went on to interpret Old Testament Scriptures beginning with Moses and all the prophets concerning the Christ. They were amazed at his teachings and eventually recognized the stranger as the resurrected Jesus.

    I would have loved to have been on that road walking and talking with the Lord. Wouldn't you?

However, in a sense, we are there having everything explained to us. Today we have the blessing of God's Word, which fully presents our redeemer, Jesus Christ. Sometimes the road leads to unexpected places. The disciples walking along that ancient path expected to arrive simply at their home in Emmaus. But the road actually took them to a new level of faith in Jesus. What happened on the path made all the difference. You see, whenever we encounter Jesus along the way, the destination always changes. We want to allow the Lord to set the course and walk with us as we travel home. Where are the roads taking you? Is Jesus a stranger or do you recognize him as Lord?

It's only when we walk with the Lord along the road of life that we get to where we really want to go. That's the message we want our community to hear.

Devotional Thought 9
Start Something You Can't Finish

"For no one can lay a foundation other than that which is laid, which is Jesus Christ." (1 Corinthians 3:11)

In 1 Corinthians 3:1-17, the apostle Paul is admonishing the church of Christ in ancient Corinth for their divisiveness, factionalism, and party spirit. He employs three metaphors in order to facilitate a corrective to their dysfunctional thinking. He uses agricultural (3:6-9b), architectural (3:9c-15), and temple (3:16-17) metaphors to make a spiritual point about Christian ministry. The overarching idea is that Christian ministry is a work of God. Who are we to mess it up and take credit for that which is not ours? Furthermore, Paul is saying we are to find our role or function in the body of Christ and do our part to serve faithfully and reflect the holiness of God.

Those who lead in Christian ministry are "God's fellow workers" (3:9a) who are part of a glorious process. One of the most important insights about the Christian ministry is this: We will not finish what we begin. This is not to say we will never set goals and reach them or that we will never complete plans and programs. It means Christian ministry must be seen in the context of faithfulness extended from generation to generation until Christ returns to claim his bride. This progressive idea of planting, watering, and increase pictures a lesson about generational fidelity. In other words, you come into the kingdom standing upon the faith of those who came before you, and then you are tasked with the mission to maintain that faith and groom others to take it up when you depart. Our job is not to reap glory. That's God's part.

The agent of all true gospel ministry is God himself. Church leaders, let me challenge you to start what you yourselves will never finish. Others will come and build on the foundation you lay. Even as the Lord grants opportunity to sow seed, we'll spend much of our lives and ministries watering. The Christian ministry is not a career. It is a calling that originates in the sovereign majesty of God and is concluded only by the next advent of Jesus Christ. The mission of church leaders, and of us all, is to be faithful to our divine calling.

Devotional Thought 10
The Lord Is In His Holy Temple

"But the LORD is in his holy temple;
let all the earth keep silence before him."
(Habakkuk 2:20)

The Old Testament book of Habakkuk spotlights the holiness of God while also shining light upon the unfaithfulness of humanity. The prophet Habakkuk longs for justice and complains to God who he thinks is being mysterious in his judgments (1:12-13). The proclamation that "the righteous shall live by his faith" (2:4) pictures an unwavering hold to the Word of God against all contrary opponents. Finally, after a series of woes -or curses- pronounced on wickedness, Habakkuk comes to the heart of the confusion (2:18-20). He mocks the foolishness of trusting in self for salvation and points the hearers of his message to a powerful declaration: "The LORD is in his holy temple; let all the earth keep silence before him" (2:20).

Then Habakkuk pours out his prayer as an exclamation of his belief in God's ability to always do the right thing. When confronted with the sovereign majesty of God, Habakkuk is undone. "I hear, and my body trembles; my lips quiver at the sound; rottenness enters into my bones; my legs tremble beneath me"

(3:16a). He concludes by declaring his trust in the Lord (3:16b) and rejoices in God's strength.

This prophecy has significance for Christians today. We too are often baffled by the confusion and chaos we encounter in life. We know we should live by faith, but it's so easy to get distracted. Then we default to a kind of self-trust that engenders pseudo-strength. What we need in times of trouble is to look to the Lord who is still in his holy temple and sovereign in his workings. We must not look to ourselves for strength in times of need because we will always let ourselves down. Rather, we look to God who is well able to supply our every need. When we look to him in faith, our complaints are silenced. Keeping silence before him means we have learned to trust in God and we look to his holiness as sure footing along life's pathway.

Devotional Thought 11
Equipping

> "Rather, speaking the truth in love, we are to grow up in every way into him who is the head, into Christ, from whom the whole body, joined and held together by every joint with which it is equipped, when each part is working properly, makes the body grow so that it builds itself up in love."
>
> (Ephesians 4:15-16)

Our desire is that every member be equipped for service in the kingdom of God. In Ephesians 4:11-16, we have a picture of a healthy church. A church where "the whole body, joined and held together by every joint with which it is equipped, when each part is working properly, makes the body grow so that it builds itself up in love" (vs. 16). Notice that the "whole body" is "equipped" for the purpose of up-building. We want to be more than comfortable Christians content to sit and stare. Rather, we want to be a church body that is alive and functioning faithfully in the work of serving God.

David did not go up against Goliath empty-handed. Rather, he took the tools and skills that were unique to him and used them to defeat a mighty enemy. He was equipped with just what was needed to accomplish the mission. Likewise, each member in the church is to take up his or her unique God-given resources and skills. God equips us with strength (Psalm 18:32) and Scripture so we "may be competent, equipped for every good work" (2 Timothy 3:17).

We want to be an equipping church. We want to be a church with unity that uses every resource and talent for God's glory. We want to be a church with zeal, eagerly engaged in the overall life of the congregation. We want to be a church with maturity that is able to carry out the work of ministry effectively. We implore every member of the church to take on the task of being equipped for faithfulness. "Now may the God of peace…equip you with everything good that you may do his will, working in us that which is pleasing in his sight" (Hebrews 13:20-21).

Devotional Thought 12
The Seven Sayings of Christ from the Cross

"So he delivered him over to them to be crucified. So they took Jesus, and he went out, bearing his own cross, to the place called the place of a skull, which in Aramaic is called Golgotha."
(John 19:16-17)

After being shuffled through a series of illegal trials all night, Jesus was condemned to die a horrible death by Roman crucifixion. He was crucified around nine o'clock in the morning. As he suffered on the cross for approximately six hours on that dark Friday -dying for you and me- He uttered seven sayings.

1) "Father, forgive them; for they know not what they do." Here is a word of **forgiveness**. Though innocent, he demonstrated divine love for even his enemies. 2) "Verily I say unto thee, Today shalt thou be with me in paradise." This is a word of **salvation**. Jesus' ministry was always characterized by compassion, and even here on the cross he was consistent in his mission to save and forgive. 3) "Woman, behold thy son!...Behold thy mother!" This is a word of **affection**. Jesus was interested in the lives of those with whom he had a particular personal relationship. He showed concern and care for his

mother, arranging for her wellbeing. 4) "Eli, Eli, lama sabachthani? that is to say, My God, my God, why hast thou forsaken me?" Here is a word of **anguish**. Jesus was embroiled in an agonizing bearing of our sin and, thus, atoned for our transgressions. 5) "I thirst." This is a word of **suffering**. The horrible thirst and bodily suffering of Jesus was very real. We must not forget his humanity and physical experiences. 6) "It is finished." This is a word of **victory**. The dynamic plan of redemption has finally been completed. There is no longer any penalty left to be paid for sins. 7) "Father, into thy hands I commend my spirit." This is a word of **contentment**. The final words of Jesus are sentiments of great faith and trust in God.

At least two things should well up within us as we reflect upon the great event of the cross. First, we are filled with humility and gratitude. This contrition of heart propels us to offer God our sincere love and service. The cross compels us to obedience. Second, we cry out with every fiber of our being, "Oh, what a Savior!"

Devotional Thought 13
Three Essential Cries of the Believer

"Because, if you confess with your mouth that Jesus is Lord and believe in your heart that God raised him from the dead, you will be saved."
(Romans 10:9)

We all know some key "cries" when there's an emergency. We know how to shout "Call 911!" If you catch on fire you know to "Stop, Drop, & Roll!" If you're the captain of the starship Enterprise you know how to shout "Shields up, Red Alert!" I would like to suggest that there are some key "cries" the Christian should know.

First, is the cry of **"Abba, Father!"** Jesus introduced the idea of a warm relationship with God in Matthew 6:9 when he taught the disciples to approach God in a personal way. God is majestic and holy; sovereign and supreme. But, he is also our tender loving heavenly father who wants us to cry out to him in our moments of despair and delight. The Aramaic "abba" conveys the notion of "father" but with added warmth and tenderness. The cry of "Abba Father" is a cry of faith. It is an appeal to God and a recognition that we are dependent upon him as children to their father (Romans 8:15; Galatians 4:6).

Second, is **"Have mercy on me, a sinner!"** This is the cry of repentance. In Luke 18:9-14 the humble worshipper stood far off in contrition and shame calling for the Lord's mercy. Jesus tells this parable to highlight the humility of this man but also to juxtapose his attitude to the egocentric man who boastfully touted his self-righteousness. Our arrogance doesn't fly with God. We must approach him with an attitude of respect, recognizing his holiness and our sinfulness.

Third, is the cry of **"Jesus is Lord!"** In Romans 10:9 we see this as the cry of confession. The supreme name that bows our knees and reveals God is Jesus Christ (Philippians 2:9,10). When we are confronted at Judgment by the Almighty we had better know the name of our Lord. Also, if we confess Jesus as Lord with our mouths then we need to be living in a way that outwardly reflects our trust in his lordship.

When you need to cry out to God, but need help with the words; try these suggestions. The cry of faith—"Abba Father!" The cry of repentance—"Have mercy on me a sinner!" And the cry of confession—"Jesus is Lord!"

Devotional Thought 14
Evangelism Matters

> "And he arose and came to his father.
> But while he was still a long way off,
> his father saw him and felt compassion,
> and ran and embraced him and kissed him."
> (Luke 15:20)

Jesus taught in Luke 15 three parables with a common theme. He tells about a lost sheep (vs. 3-6) and the shepherd who leaves the flock to go in search of the one, a lost coin (vs. 8,9) and the woman who sweeps the house in a diligent search, and a lost son who squanders his life in wasteful living (vs. 11-24). Jesus was trying to teach the people about spiritual matters and so he used these simple stories to convey the significance of salvation. Today, we need the same lessons on evangelism and salvation. Evangelism involves sharing the soul-saving good news about Jesus Christ.

Consider these points from this parable by Jesus: First, each person matters greatly to God. Spiritually lost people stir the heart of God. We don't meet anyone, whether on the street or in a store, who is not the object of God's love. We need to make sure that we are genuinely concerned about the lost. Second, it warrants an all out search. The individuals in the stories went on a quest for that which was lost. Likewise, evangelism is something we should be passionate about. Each Christian should be eagerly looking for opportunities to tell others about Christ and His church. Third, God welcomes the saved to Him. In each parable, there is rejoicing and gladness when that which was lost is found. Likewise, there is a cosmic celebration when a lost sinner comes to God in submissive, obedient faith (vs. 7,10).

Evangelism is a vital part of what we are to be doing as Christians and yet so often we allow fear to stifle this core ministry. We desperately need to get energized about effectively sharing the gospel. We need a fresh commitment to have the kind of compassion exemplified by God which motivates us to partner with him in seeking and saving the lost (Luke 19:10). Let us work to better develop the spiritual skill of speaking the gospel because evangelism matters.

Devotional Thought 15
Our Attitude Toward the Word of God

"For the word of God is living and active, sharper than any two-edged sword."
(Hebrews 4:12)

Consider the power of Scripture. We affirm that the Bible is effective and well able to accomplish what it was designed to do. When we authentically engage with the Word of God, we can't help but be changed and molded. The Bible is powerful and it changes lives for the better. Hebrews 4:12 pictures Scripture as a living instrument capable of piercing our inner-most being. Let me put it this way: reading the Word of God is not the safest activity in which we can engage. This Word jabs at us and cuts us, forcing a response. You see, we don't read the Bible just for information. Rather, we engage with it for transformation. This is a book that will change our lives if we allow it to. The Bible is effective in accomplishing its divine function of changing lives.

Believers are challenged to adopt a healthy attitude toward the Word of God. The Bible is inspired, inerrant, sufficient, authoritative, and effective. It is the life changing, truth revealing, inspired Word of God. Let us cherish and love God's revealed message to the world. Let us diligently seek to live a life that honors God's Word as the true guide it is.

Appendix 2 – Sample Sermon
Draw Near to God

We have two wonderful young children. Something that comes along with having young kids is the reality of daily catastrophes. Something will always happen that causes one of them to erupt into tears and come running to my wife or me with arms outstretched. When one of our children is standing in front of us with red eyes filled with wet tears, and arms reaching for the heavens, we don't just stand there and ignore them. Of course not! We gently pick them up and try to soothe their discomfort. You know what happens every time? They calm down and the catastrophe is averted. Just like when a child is upset and crying and longing to be lifted up into the safe and secure arms of a parent where there is peace, so God our tender loving heavenly father, is willing to lift us up into His everlasting arms and provide peace and security. For those who are His children, God offers nearness.

In James 4:7-10 we have a powerful description of how we can draw near to God. From time to time we all need to be renewed in our relationship with the Lord. One of our great goals in the Christian faith is to maintain a close individual faith-filled relationship with God Almighty. After all, nearness to God is the basic call and claim of biblical faith. The passage at hand has many tender images but it also has some fierce military-like language. We want to be sure to note each as we go through this scripture together.

Let's look carefully at the text. James is interested in teaching about straight forward faith-filled living that practically plays out in a life of zealous obedience to God. In the context of this passage James is issuing a solemn warning against worldliness. Notice our text: "Submit yourselves therefore to God. Resist the devil, and he will flee from you. Draw near to God, and he will draw near to you. Cleanse your hands, you sinners, and purify your hearts, you double minded. Be wretched and mourn and weep. Let your laughter be turned to mourning and your joy to gloom. Humble yourselves before the Lord, and he will exalt you."

What we need to notice first is the sharp contrast that James presents in verse seven; "Submit yourselves therefore to God. Resist the Devil, and he will flee from you." When it comes to our relationship with God we should *submit* but when it comes to our relationship with Satan we are to *resist*. To draw near to God we must resist the Devil. However, first note this idea of submitting to God. The picture is one of wrestling with an opponent. When one is down and defeated he must "submit." However, in our progression of faith we do not submit in humiliation but with humility. There is a difference. Perhaps the better image, what I think James intends here, is a loyal soldier submitting his service and pledging his allegiance to his captain. Likewise, we submit to God in the sense that we turn to him and recognize his leadership in our lives.

The contrast to submitting to God is this notion of resisting the Devil. This means we must deflect his advances. He has many devices for temptation at his disposal but we need to mount a defense against his spiritual onslaught. James has just said, in verse four that, there cannot be split allegiance. Now he dramatically paints the picture of two opposing forces. We must choose which side we're on. Jesus said something of the same sentiment when he said, "No one can serve two masters…" (Matthew 6:24).

Not only does James present a lesson in contrast but he also gives us a lesson in comparison. There is a mutual drawing near. "Draw near to God, and he will draw near to you" (vs. 8a). The image of "drawing near" is found in the approach of the priest to God in the temple for worship and sacrifice under the Levitical system. Under the Christian system all obedient believers are priests who are to draw near to God. What's so remarkable is, as we draw near to God in righteousness, he reciprocates by drawing near to us. God is gladly willing to abide and be near those who choose him. The story of the prodigal son offers a splendid example of what James is talking about. When the prodigal repented and went back to his father's house, "But while he was still a long way off, his father saw him and felt compassion, and ran and embraced him and kissed him" (Luke 15:20). When we, in repentance, draw near to God, He is lovingly longing to draw near to us. The fundamental longing of every human heart is for the Father's embrace.

But an important question is raised: How can we draw near to God? The text says by getting rid of our sins. Sin separates us from God. Isaiah 59:2 says, "Your iniquities have made a separation between you and your God, and your sins have hidden his face from you." The apostle Paul in Ephesians 2:12-13 says, "Remember that you were at that time separated from Christ, alienated from the commonwealth of Israel and strangers to the covenants of promise, having no hope and without God in the world. But now in Christ Jesus you who once were far off have been brought near by the blood of Christ."

When our sin is removed by the blood of Christ and we are forgiven, we may then approach God. Verses eight and nine of James 4 highlight this somber scene. "Cleanse your hands, you sinners, and purify your hearts, you double minded. Be wretched and mourn and weep. Let your laughter be turned to mourning and your joy to gloom." James says an outflowing of this contrition comes from realizing the ugliness and filth of sin.

Sin and Satan are the terrible enemies that face the Christian on the spiritual battlefield. The combat vocabulary James uses is more readily apparent in the broader context. In fact, in verses seven through ten (only four verses), there are ten imperatival verb tense usages. This barrage of imperatives was no doubt obvious to the original Greek reader and would have stood out as heavily emphasizing careful compliance. Furthermore, the point James is emphasizing overall in verses one through ten seems to be that "whoever desires to be a friend of the world makes himself an enemy of God" (vs. 4).

Let me illustrate. In Afghanistan our military soldiers are not wandering around the cities saying, "Oh, look at that architecture." or "Wow, let me sit and stare at the Middle East sky for a while." Of course they're not doing that. Instead, they must be constantly alert and focused on the serious task of defending themselves and watching for attack. Too many Christians are staring at worldly pleasures and saying, "Wow, let me enjoy that for a while." Don't you know we're in a spiritual war? James is issuing a call to action and a plea for us to resist the enemy and commit ourselves to the side of faith. James teaches that submissive, obedient faith must command our focus. We need to be somber about this serious task and not flippantly out of focus.

Let me make a nuts-and bolts practical point of application here. An important part of our approach to God involves service in his presence. If we are going to be close to God then we must be characterized by righteousness. Evil does not stand side by side with good. Competing forces do not fellowship on the field of battle. Trying to have one foot in the world with sin and one foot in the church with holiness does not work. We must strive for faithfulness. This faithful service involves spiritual growth. Spiritual growth involves things like Bible study. You must adopt a regular routine of reading that you might be near to God through his Word.

Through Scripture, God reaches out to us to conform and mold us into something more akin to Christ. A lot comes down to the doctrine of revelation. God really has spoken and his Word really is his will revealed. If we truly believe that then we are obligated for the teaching the telling of it (Consider carefully 2 Timothy 3:14-4:5). If this is the Word of God then we must study it, we must preach it, we must labor over it and do our best to figure out what it says, and then we must live it. Those are the inescapable implications of divine revelation. If God truly speaks through his Word then we are obligated to listen and obey. The foundation for the Christian faith is Jesus Christ. And where do we learn of Christ but through the Bible?

Furthermore, faithfulness to God also means behavior modification wherein we become more Christ-like. Do not compartmentalize your life into different sections of behavior but be consistent in your Christianity.

The text culminates in verse ten with the explicit result of exaltation flowing from the cause of humbling before the Lord. "Humble yourselves before the Lord, and he will exalt you" (vs. 10). I see a remarkable reversal produced by God. When we humble ourselves and come lowly before the Lord, he will bring about a great reversal and exalt us. Humility carries with it the idea of spiritually bowing down before God and acquiescing to his ways.

Perhaps one of the most practical expressions of "drawing near to God" is prayer. We often use the expression "let us go to God in prayer." That is a valid image. With Christ as our mediator we are carried to the heights of heaven and permitted to petition the Creator of the Universe. If we carefully reflect upon this image we will be compelled to be more reverent, thoughtful, and humble in the wording and delivery of our prayers. In prayer there is power (God answers prayer providentially) and presence (we go before the very throne of God).

Finally, there is exaltation from God. A progression is detectable: from submitting to God, to a mutual drawing near, then "washing" the hands and purifying the heart, and finally, exaltation from God. God is a great God of reversal and well able to turn our gloom into glory.

It is truly amazing that we have opportunity to commit ourselves to the joyful task of drawing near to God. What a tremendous privilege to be invited to approach our Creator. Furthermore, he promises to approach us in this process of reciprocal drawing near, wherein the gap between us is daily diminished. As we consider this opportunity may we seriously commit to reaffirm our relationship with God. God is not reached by roaming aimlessly, depending on luck to get us to him. Rather, we must deliberately go in the direction he has set for us in order to successfully reach him. Are you drawing near... or wandering away? Can you truly say, "But for me it is good to be near God; I have made the Lord God my refuge, that I may tell of all your works" (Psalms 73:28).

Just like when a child is upset and crying and longing to be lifted up into the safe secure arms of a parent where there is peace, so God our tender loving heavenly Father is willing to lift us up into his everlasting arms and provide peace and security. For those who are his children, God offers nearness.

Appendix 3

BIBLIOGRAPHY

Books

Achtemeier, Elizabeth. *Preaching from the Old Testament*. Louisville: Westminster / John Knox Press, 1989.

_____. *The Old Testament and the Proclamation of the Gospel*. Philadelphia: Westminster Press, 1973.

Akin, Daniel L., David L. Allen, and Ned L. Mathews, ed. *Text-Driven Preaching: God's Word at the Heart of Every Sermon*. Nashville: B&H Academic, 2010.

Allen, Ronald J., and John C. Holbert. *Holy Root Holy Branches: Christian Preaching from the Old Testament*. Nashville: Abingdon Press, 1995.

Anderson, Kenton C. *Choosing to Preach: A Comprehensive Introduction to Sermon Options and Structures*. Grand Rapids: Zondervan, 2006.

Barth, Karl. *Homiletics*. Louisville: Westminster / John Knox Press, 1991.

Beale, G.K. *Commentary on the New Testament Use of the Old Testament*. Grand Rapids: Baker Academic, 2002.

Bonhoeffer, Dietrich. *Worldly Preaching*, ed. Clyde E. Fant, New York: Thomas Nelson, 1975.

Borland, James. *Christ in the Old Testament*, Rev. and expanded ed. Fearn, Ross-shire: Christian Focus, 2010.

Broadus, John A. *On the Preparation and Delivery of Sermons*. Rev. ed. New York: Harper & Row Pub., 1944.

Brown Jr., H.C., H. Gordon Clinard, Jesse J. Northcutt, and Al Fasol. *Steps to the Sermon: An Eight-Step Plan for Preaching with Confidence*. Rev. ed. Nashville: B&H Pub., 1996.

Buttrick, David. *Homiletic: Moves and Structures*. Philadelphia: Fortress Press, 1987.

Chapell, Bryan. *Christ-Centered Preaching: Redeeming the Expository Sermon*. Grand Rapids: Baker Books, 1994.

Clowney, Edmund P. *Preaching Christ in All of Scripture*. Wheaton: Crossway Books, 2003.

_____. *The Unfolding Mystery: Discovering Christ in the Old Testament*. Phillipsburg: P&R Pub., 1990.

Cahill, Dennis M. *The Shape of Preaching: Theory and Practice in Sermon Design*. Grand Rapids: Baker Books, 2007.

Chapell, Bryan. *Christ-Centered Preaching: Redeeming the Expository Sermon*. Grand Rapids: Baker Books, 1994.

Craddock, Fred B. *As One without Authority*. St. Lewis: Chalice Press, 2001.

_____. *Preaching*. Nashville: Abingdon Press, 2010.

Danker, Frederick William, ed. *A Greek-English Lexicon of the New Testament and other Early Christian Literature*. 3rd ed. Chicago: Univ. of Chicago Press, 2000.

Decker, Bert. *You've God to Be Believed to Be Heard*. Rev. ed. New York: St. Martin's Press, 2008.

Dever, Mark. *Nine Marks of a Healthy Church*. Wheaton: Crossway Books, 2004.

Erickson, Richard J. *A Beginnger's Guide to New Testament Exegesis: Taking the Fear Out of Critical Method*. Downers Grove: InterVarsity Press, 2005.

Fee, Gordon D. *New Testament Exegesis: A Handbook for Students and Pastors*. Rev. ed. Louisville: Westminster / John Knox Press, 1993.

Ferrell, James. *The Hidden Christ: Beneath the Surface of the Old Testament*. Salt Lake City: Deseret Book, 2009.

France, R.T. *Jesus and the Old Testament: His Application of Old Testament Passages to Himself and His Mission*. London: Tyndale, 1971.

Friedrich, Gerhard. *Theological Dictionary of the New Testament*, ed. Gerhard Kittel, vol. 3. Grand Rapids: Eerdmans, 1965.

Goldsworthy, Graeme. *Preaching the Whole Bible as Christian Scripture: The Application of Biblical Theology to Expository Preaching*. Grand Rapids: Eerdmans, 2000.

_____. *According To Plan: The Unfolding Revelation of God in the Bible*. Downers Grove: InterVarsity Press, 1991.

Gordon, T. David. *Why Johnny Can't Preach: The Media Have Shaped the Messengers*. Phillipsburg: P&R Pub., 2009.

Gowan, Donald. *Reclaiming the Old Testament for the Christian Pulpit*. Atlanta: John Knox Press, 1980.

Graves, Mike, ed. *What's the Matter with Preaching Today?* Louisville: Westminster / John Knox Press, 2004.

Greidanus, Sidney. *Preaching Christ from Genesis: Foundations for Expository Sermons.* Grand Rapids: Eerdmans, 2007.

_____. *Preaching Christ from the Old Testament : A Contemporary Hermeneutical Method.* Grand Rapids: Eerdmans Pub., 1999.

_____. *The Modern Preacher and the Ancient Text: Interpreting and Preaching Biblical Literature.* Grand Rapids: Eerdmans Pub., 1988.

Grenville, J.R. Kent. *He Began with Moses: Preaching the Old Testament Today.* Nottingham: Inter-Varsity Press, 2010.

Grenville, J.R. Kent, Paul J. Kissling, and Laurence A. Turner, eds. *Reclaiming the Old Testament for Christian Preaching.* Downers Grove: IVP Academic, 2010.

Guthrie, Donald. *Tyndale New Testament Commentaries: The Pastoral Epistles.* Revised Ed. Grand Rapids: Inter-Varsity Press, 1990.

Holbert, John C. *Preaching Old Testament: Proclamation & Narrative in the Hebrew Bible.* Nashville: Abingdon Press, 1991.

Holland, Thomas H. *Encouraging Expository Preaching.* Brentwood: Penmann Books, 2000.

E.D. Hirsch. *Validity in Interpretation.* New Haven: Yale Univ. Press, 1967.

Johnson, Dennis E. *Him We Proclaim: Preaching Christ from All the Scriptures.* Phillipsburg: P&R Publishing, 2007.

Kaiser, Walter C., Jr. *The Majesty of God in the Old Testament: A Guide for Preaching and Teaching.* Grand Rapids: Baker Academic, 2007.

_____. *Toward An Exegetical Theology: Biblical Exegesis for Preaching and Teaching.* Grand Rapids: Baker Academic, 1981.

_____. *Toward an Old Testament Theology.* Grand Rapids: Zondervan Pub., 1978.

Klein, George L., ed. *Reclaiming the Prophetic Mantle: Preaching the Old Testament Faithfully.* Nashville: Broadman Press, 1993.

Koller, Charles W. *How to Preach Without Notes.* Grand Rapids: Baker Books, 1964.

Lawson, Steven J. *Famine in the Land: A Passionate Call for Expository Preaching.* Chicago: Moody Publishers, 2003.

Love, Bill. *The Core Gospel: On Restoring the Crux of the Matter.* Abilene: ACU Press, 1992.

Lowry, Eugene L. *The Homiletical Plot: The Sermon as Narrative Art Form.* Louisville: Westminster/John Knox Press, 2001.

Mathewson, Steven D. *The Art of Preaching Old Testament Narrative.* Grand Rapids: Baker Academic, 2002.

Mathis, Shawn D., ed. *Man of God: Essays on the Life and Work of the Preacher.* Nashville: Gospel Advocate Co., 1996.

McDill, Wayne. *Twelve Essential Skills for Great Preaching.* 2nd ed. Nashville: B&H Academic, 2006.

McQuoid, Stephen. *The Beginner's Guide to Expository Preaching.* Great Britain: Christian Focus Pub., 2002.

Mohler, R. Albert. *He is Not Silent: Preaching in a Postmodern World.* Chicago: Moody Press, 2008.

Montgomery, John Warwick. ed. *God's Inerrant Word: An International Symposium on the Trustworthiness of Scripture.* Newburgh: Trinity Press, 1974.

_____. *Where Is History Going?: A Christian Response to Secular Philosophies of History.* Newburgh: Trinity Press, 1961.

Moss, Michael C. *The College Press NIV Commentary: 1,2 Timothy & Titus.* Joplin: College Press Pub. Co., 1994.

Newton, Derek. *And The Word Became A Sermon: A Practical Guide to Biblical Expository Preaching.* Glasgow: Bell & Bain, 2003.

Osborne, Grant R. *The Hermeneutical Spiral: A Comprehensive Introduction to Biblical Interpretation.* Downers Grove: IVP Academic, 2006.

Osborn, Ronald E. *Folly of God: The Rise of Christian Preaching.* St. Louis: Chalice Press, 1999.

Porter, Stanley E. ed. *A Handbook to the Exegesis of the New Testament.* Boston: Brill Academic Pub., 1997.

Quicke, Michael J. *360 Degree Preaching: Hearing, Speaking, and Living the Word.* Grand Rapids: Baker Academic, 2003.

Radmacher, Earl D. and Robert D. Preus, eds. *Hermeneutics, Inerrancy & the Bible.* Grand Rapids: Zondervan Publishing House, 1984.

Rydelnik, Michael. *The Messianic Hope: Is the Hebrew Bible Really Messianic?* Nashville: B&H Academic, 2010.

Richard, Ramesh. *Scripture Sculpture: A Do-It-Yourself Manual for Biblical Preaching.* Grand Rapids: Baker Books, 1995.

Robertson, A.T. *Word Pictures in the New Testament.* Vol. 4. Nashville: Broadman Press, 1931.

Robinson, Haddon W. *Biblical Preaching: The Development and Delivery of Expository Messages.* Grand Rapids: Baker Book House, 1980.

_____ and Craig Brian Larson. eds. *The Art and Craft of Biblical Preaching: A Comprehensive Resource for Today's Communicators.* Grand Rapids: Zondervan Press, 2005.

Shaddix, Jim. *The Passion Driven Sermon: Changing the Way Pastors Preach and Congregations Listen.* Nashville: B&H Pub., 2003.

Spurgeon, C.H. *Lectures to My Students.* Grand Rapids: Zondervan Pub., 1954.

Stanley, Andy. *Communicating for a Change: Seven Keys to Irresistible Communication.* Sisters: Multnomah Pub., 2006.

Stone, Dave. ed. *Refining Your Style: Learning from Respected Communicators.* Loveland: Group Pub., 2004.

Stuart, Douglas. *Old Testament Exegesis: A Handbook for Students and Pastors.* 3rd ed. Louisville: Westminster/John Knox Press, 2001.

Stein, Robert H. *A Basic Guide to Interpreting the Bible: Playing by the Rules.* Grand Rapids: Baker Books, 1994.

Stott, John. *Between Two Worlds: The Challenge of Preaching Today.* Grand Rapids: Eerdmans Pub. Co., 1982

_____. *The Message of 2 Timothy: The Bible Speak Today Series.* Downers Grove: Inter-Varsity Press, 1973.

Sunukjian, Donald R. *Invitation to Biblical Preaching: Proclaiming Truth with Clarity and Relevance.* Grand Rapids: Kregel Pub., 2007.

Thompson, James W. *Preaching Like Paul: Homiletical Wisdom for Today.* Louisville: Westminster/John Knox Press, 2001.

Vines, Jerry and Jim Shaddix. *Power in the Pulpit: How to Prepare and Deliver Expository Sermons.* Chicago: Moody Press, 1999.

Wallace, Daniel B. *Greek Grammar Beyond the Basics: An Exegetical Syntax of the New Testament.* Grand Rapids: Zondervan Pub., 1996.

Webb, Stephen H. *The Divine Voice: Christian Proclamation and the Theology of Sound.* Grand Rapids: Brazos Press, 2004.

Wells, C. Richard and A. Boyd Luter. *Inspired Preaching: A Survey of Preaching Found in the New Testament.* Nashville: B&H Pub., 2002.

Wright, Christopher. *Knowing Jesus through the Old Testament.* Downers Grove: InterVarsity Press, 1995.

Wright, N.T. *Scripture and the Authority of God: How to Read the Bible Today.* New York: Harper Collins Pub., 2011.

York Hershael W. and Bert Decker. *Preaching With Bold Assurnace: A Solid and Enduring Approach to Engaging Exposition.* Nashville: B&H Pub. Group, 2003.

Zerwick, Max and Mary Grosvenor. *A Grammatical Analysis of the Greek New Testament.* 5th Rev. ed. Rome: Editrice Pontificio Istituto Biblico, 1996.

Book Chapters

Bloesch, Donald G. "A Christological Hermeneutic: Crisis and Conflict in Hermeneutics." In *The Use of the Bible in Theology: Evangelical Options*. Ed. Robert K. Johnston. Atlanta: John Knox, 1985. Pp. 78-102.

Duduit, Michael. "The Church's Need for Old Testament Preaching." In *Reclaiming the Prophetic Mantle*. Ed. George L. Klein. Nashville: Broadman, 1992. Pp. 9-16.

Eichrodt, Walther. "Is Typological Exegesis an Appropriate Method?" In *Essays on Old Testament Hermeneutics*. Ed. Claus Westermann. Richmond: John Knox, 1963. Pp. 224-245.

Lutzer, Erwin W. "A Response to Homiletics and Hermeneutics." In *Hermeneutics, Inerrancy, and the Bible*. Ed. Earl D. Radmacher and Robert D. Preus. Grand Rapids: Zondervan, 1984. Pp. 833-837.

Vischer, Wilhelm. "Everywhere the Scripture Is About Christ Alone." In *The Old Testament and Christian Faith*. Ed. B.W. Anderson. New York: Harper and Row, 1963. Pp. 90-101.

York, Hershael. "Communication Theory and Text-Driven Preaching." In *Text Driven Preaching: God's Word at the Heart of Every Sermon.* Eds. Daniel L. Akin, David L. Allen, and Ned L. Mathews. Nashville: B&H Academic, 2010. Pp. 221-242.

Articles

Baird, William R. "Biblical Preaching as Incarnational Preaching." *Lexington Theological Quarterly* 16, no. 3 (July 1, 1981): 105-115.

Baker, David L. "Typology and the Christian Use of the Old Testament." *Scottish Journal of Theology* 29 (1976): 137-157.

Barr, George K. "Preaching the Old Testament." *Expository Times* 118:1 (2006): 12-18.

Beale, G.K. "Did Jesus and the Apostles Preach the Right Doctrine From the Wrong Texts? Revisiting the Debate Seventeen Years Later in the Light of Peter Enn's Book, Inspiration and Incarnation." *Themelios* 32:1 (2006): 18-43.

Bresee, Floyd. "Expository Preaching." *Ministry Magazine* (1955; Digitally Reprinted, 1994).

Ericson, Norman R. "The New Testament Use of the Old Testament: A Kerygmatic Approach." *Journal of the Evangelical Theological Society* 30 (1987): 337-342.

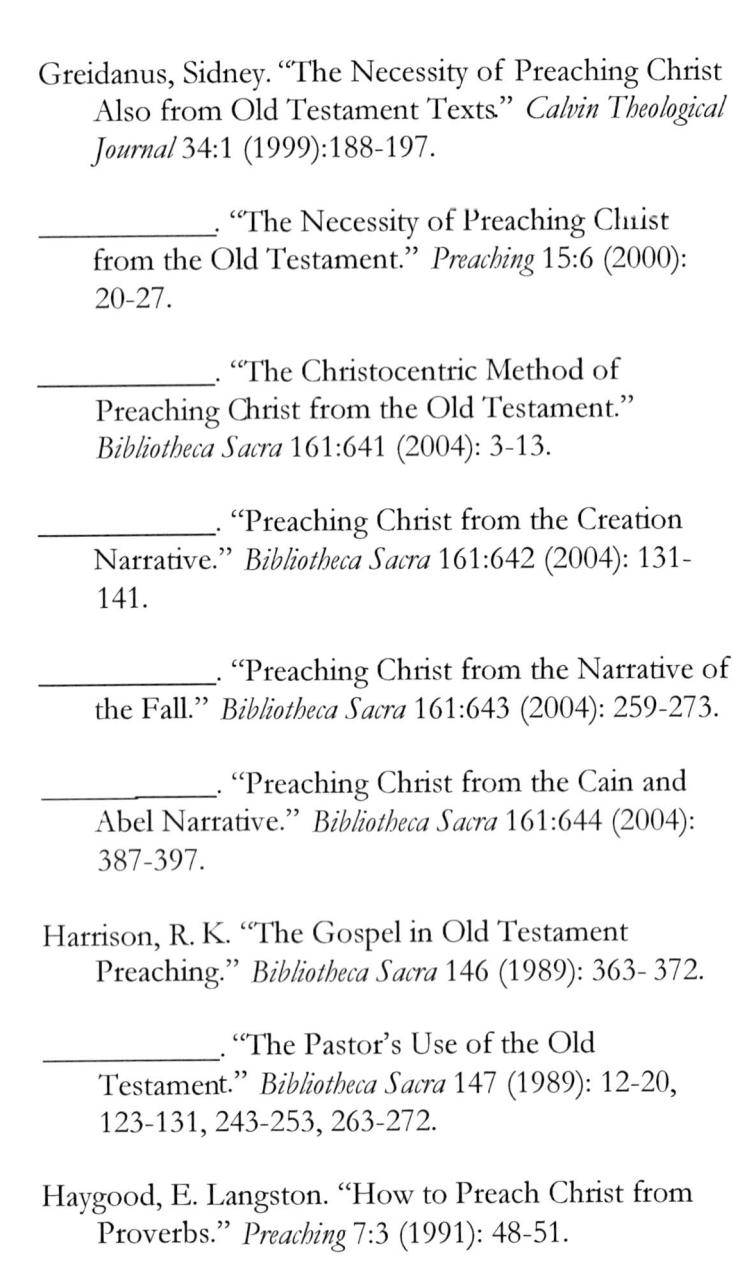

Greidanus, Sidney. "The Necessity of Preaching Christ Also from Old Testament Texts." *Calvin Theological Journal* 34:1 (1999):188-197.

_____. "The Necessity of Preaching Christ from the Old Testament." *Preaching* 15:6 (2000): 20-27.

_____. "The Christocentric Method of Preaching Christ from the Old Testament." *Bibliotheca Sacra* 161:641 (2004): 3-13.

_____. "Preaching Christ from the Creation Narrative." *Bibliotheca Sacra* 161:642 (2004): 131-141.

_____. "Preaching Christ from the Narrative of the Fall." *Bibliotheca Sacra* 161:643 (2004): 259-273.

_____. "Preaching Christ from the Cain and Abel Narrative." *Bibliotheca Sacra* 161:644 (2004): 387-397.

Harrison, R. K. "The Gospel in Old Testament Preaching." *Bibliotheca Sacra* 146 (1989): 363-372.

_____. "The Pastor's Use of the Old Testament." *Bibliotheca Sacra* 147 (1989): 12-20, 123-131, 243-253, 263-272.

Haygood, E. Langston. "How to Preach Christ from Proverbs." *Preaching* 7:3 (1991): 48-51.

Longenecker, Richard N. "Who Is the Prophet Talking About: Some Reflections on the New Testament's Use in the Old." *Themelios* 13 (1987): 4-8.

Murray, David. "Bright Shadows: Preaching Christ from the Old Testament, part 1." *Puritan Reformed Journal* 1 (Jan. 2009): 23-33.

_____. "Bright Shadows: Preaching Christ from the Old Testament, part 2." *Puritan Reformed Journal* 1 (July 2009): 5-11.

Roehrs, Walter R. "The Typological Use of the Old Testament in the New Testament." *Concordia Journal* 10:6 (1984): 204-216.

Schreiner, Thomas R. "Christ in the Old Testament." *Southern Seminary Magazine* 79:2 (Spring 2011): 36-37.

Selvaggio, Anthony T. "An Answer to the Challenge of Preaching the Old Testament: An Historical and Theological Examination of the Redemptive-Historical Approach." *Confessional Presbyterian* 5 (2009): 170-184.

Smith, Steven W. "Christology of Preaching." *Southwestern Journal of Theology* 50, no. 2 (March 1, 2008): 134-145.

Stitzinger, James F. "The History of Expository Preaching." *The Master's Seminary Journal* 3/1 (Spring 1992): 5-32.

About the Author

Paul N. Merideth grew up in Lawrenceburg, Tennessee. He has been in full-time preaching ministry since 1999 and has worked with churches in Tennessee, New Mexico, and Kentucky. Paul has a B.A. from Freed-Hardeman University, an M.A. from Trinity Theological Seminary, and a M.Div. from The Southern Baptist Theological Seminary where he is currently a Ph.D. student in Theology. Paul and his wife Amanda have two children, Emma and Thomas.